best ever
 one pot

p

This is a Parragon Publishing Book
First published in 2003

Parragon Publishing
Queen Street House
4 Queen Street
Bath BA1 1HE
United Kingdom

Created and produced by
The Bridgewater Book Company Ltd,
Lewes, East Sussex

Photographer David Jordan
Home Economist Judy Williams
The publishers would like to thank Moulinex for lending the food processor
and Tower Pans for supplying the stainless steel pans and skillets

ISBN:1-40541-689-0

Printed in China

NOTE

This book uses imperial and metric measurements. Follow the same units
of measurement throughout; do not mix imperial and metric. All spoon
measurements are level: teaspoons are assumed to be 5 ml and tablespoons are
assumed to be 15 ml. Unless otherwise stated, milk is assumed to be whole milk,
eggs and individual vegetables such as potatoes are medium, and pepper is freshly
ground black pepper.

The times given for each recipe are an approximate guide only because
the preparation times may differ according to the techniques used by
different people and the cooking times may vary as a result of the type of
oven used. Ovens should be preheated to the specified temperature. If using
a fan-assisted oven, check the manufacturer's instructions for adjusting the time
and temperature. The preparation times include chilling and marinating times,
where appropriate.

The nutritional information provided for each recipe is per serving or per portion.
Optional ingredients, variations or serving suggestions have not been included
in the calculations.

Recipes using raw or very lightly cooked eggs should be avoided
by infants, the elderly, pregnant women, convalescents, and anyone
suffering from an illness.

contents

introduction

With today's hectic lifestyles, it is all too easy to resort to unhealthy and expensive takeaways and convenience foods. For a more economical and healthier alternative that is almost as easy, why not try one-pot meals for parties, Sunday lunches, or family suppers? One-pot meals include everything from traditional soups and bakes to international dishes from Persia, Mexico, and the Mediterranean, and delicious alcoholic desserts—you will find a dish for every occasion.

Preparing food at home can give you a great sense of satisfaction, but it can seem something of a chore, and clearing up afterwards is often very tedious. If you have a busy life, one-pot meals may well be exactly what you need. Cook meals in batches and freeze, then warm in the microwave when you need them and relax for a few minutes. Running a household, holding down a job, and feeding the family can be difficult to balance, and one-pot meals are the ideal time-saving solution. They make busy lives easier, create less washing-up, make less mess in the kitchen, and involve less chopping and peeling than many other dishes.

One-pot dishes also save on washing-up—they eliminate the need for a pan, skillet, casserole, and several serving dishes—most one-pot dishes can be served straight from the cooking pot. Try to find an attractive set of casseroles so that you can serve from the pot at the table, even when you have guests. One more advantage of not using serving dishes is that the food is kept piping hot, which saves you the fuss of warming plates in the oven beforehand.

Many one-pot meals can be frozen. Make them in large batches and freeze in family or single serving portions, depending on your household. Casseroles and stews are great for cooking in batches: double the ingredients (making sure your pot is big enough), and when the dish is ready, simply let half of it cool, then freeze in a rigid container or freezer bag. Soups will freeze well and can be kept for up to 3 months. To thaw, simply remove from the freezer 12 hours before you require the dish and let it stand at room temperature, or remove 24 hours before and place in the refrigerator.

the spice of life

One-pot meals need never be boring. The wonderful range of recipes featured here includes traditional stews and casseroles, perfect for winter evenings and large families. There are plenty of meat dishes, such as Irish Stew (see page 67) and Pork & Sausage Bake (see page 93)—hearty favorites guaranteed to fill you up. Fish is also featured, and you could serve Goan Fish Curry (see page 128) for a weekday supper, Cod in Lemon & Parsley (see page 121) for Sunday lunch, or Swordfish with Tomatoes & Olives (see page 126) as a main meal at a dinner party. There are dishes for vegetarian families or guests, such as Risotto with Four Cheeses (see page 188), which makes a substantial lunch or dinner. Also impressive is Pasta with Garlic & Pine Nuts (see page 195), which would provide a delicious main meal for meat-eaters too. Of course, not all one-pot meals have to be wintry casseroles, stews, and pies—try Tricolor Pasta Salad (see page 194) as a summery lunch or alfresco meal, or make one of the risottos featured, such as Seafood Risotto (see page 187), for a warm picnic dish.

There are a surprising number of sweet one-pot dishes to serve for dessert. Try a substantial dish to follow a light meal—complement Risotto Primavera (see page 189) with Cinnamon & Apricot Crêpes (see page 245).

A light summer meal eaten alfresco would be perfectly complemented by Forest Fruits Granita (see page 251) or Syllabub (see page 232).

Every cuisine in the world features one-pot dishes, proving how valuable and delicious they are. One-pot cooking preserves many of the nutrients that can disappear during boiling, broiling, and roasting. They are usually cooked slowly over a long period of time, allowing the flavors and colors to mingle beautifully. Some of the recipes in this book are well known, such as Quick Clam Chowder (see page 29), Brunswick Stew (see page 96), Louisiana Rice (see page 177), and Jambalaya (see page 184). Many British favorites are featured, such as Scottish Cock-a-Leekie (see page 23), Irish Stew (see page 67), Pot-Roast Pork (see page 83), and Flummery (see page 231), for example. Other dishes are more exotic, but this does not mean that they are harder to cook, and you should not be afraid to experiment with new flavors and ingredients. Try Chinese and south-east Asian methods of cooking, such as Hot & Sour Soup (see page 39) and Sweet & Sour Shrimp (see page 148). Visit the rest of America with Mexican Turkey (see page 115) and Chili Con Carne (see page 56). Chicken Cacciatore (see page 103) is a well-known Italian dish,

while the Spanish Paella Del Mar (see page 132) is a variation on the classic chicken paella. Try one-pot dishes from Morocco, France, Thailand, Germany, and Greece and find out which cuisine suits you—you never know, it may decide where you holiday next!

equipment

Investing in good-quality equipment is important. Poor quality pans and dishes do not cook food evenly, and are difficult to clean. The most important pieces of equipment for one-pot cooking are casserole dishes, skillets, and pans. When making casseroles and pot roasts, you need a dish large enough to give the ingredients room to cook, but not so much room that they dry out.

If you are planning to cook lots of casseroles and stews, a flameproof casserole will be your best buy. A solid, heavy-bottomed casserole can be expensive, but is worth the cost, because meals will be evenly cooked and flavorsome. A cast-iron casserole is best, but remember that they are very heavy when full.

Woks, skillets, and karahis (the Indian version of a wok) are also used for one-pot dishes, especially for stir-frying. Roasting pans are also important for cooking one-pot roasts, with the vegetables sizzling in the juices from the meat. You may prefer a non-stick lining, but whatever type you choose, make sure that it is solid and large, and that the sides are of an adequate height, or you may find that cooking juices drip dangerously over the rim.

You should think about the dishes you plan to cook and, therefore, the type of pan you will find most useful. If you cook on an electric stove with a flat surface, select a wok with a flat bottom, for example. A thick, solid bottom allows an even distribution of heat. If the manufacturer's instructions tell you to season a pan before use, do so, because this improves the quality of cooking and the pan's lifespan.

You will probably already have most of the other necessary utensils, but there may be some, such as a zester, that you might need to buy. Using a zester is far easier than trying to grate lemon or orange rind and then scrape it from the inside of the grater. They are inexpensive and readily available. Cutting boards are an essential item and will last a long time. Whether you prefer wood or plastic, select a good, solid board that will not slip easily. Remember to use a separate board for raw meat. It is now thought that you should avoid cleaning utensils with anti-bacterial products, because various strains of bacteria can become completely resistant. Hot soapy water is adequate for all pans and utensils; soak them first to remove burnt food.

Measuring pitchers and cups with clear, easy-to-read numbers are essential. Although you can estimate amounts with many casseroles and stews, some dishes require exact measurements. Make sure you have a full set of imperial or metric measuring equipment and remember that the two systems are not interchangeable.

Other tools you will need include a perforated spoon for draining and serving—very valuable in one-pot cooking when you need to remove the meat ahead of the sauce. Try to find a good set of plastic utensils for non-stick surfaces or stainless steel for other dishes—these will last for years. A pestle and mortar is a necessity if you like to use fresh spices, which add a better flavor and color than ready-ground ones.

Good-quality, sharp knives make life a lot easier, saving time and increasing safety in the kitchen. You should also buy a knife sharpener—using blunt knives is dangerous. A carving knife is ideal for carving pot roasts and other joints of meat. A large chopping knife with a heavy blade is useful for a multitude of purposes, but you may find a range of different knives suits you. A paring knife is smaller and lighter and is perfect for trimming, peeling, and chopping small vegetables.

Nowadays, there are ways to speed up preparation times. For a real timesaver, invest in a food processor—a good-quality one will last for a long time. Alternatively, most major food stores now stock a range of washed, peeled, and chopped vegetables, such as carrots, baby corn cobs, and salads, as well as canned goods. Canned foods are not so fresh as the ready-prepared varieties and often have little flavor and color, but some types, such as tomatoes and pulses, are invaluable.

the pantry

Although fresh vegetables have a unique flavor and texture, there are alternatives that can make a delicious last-minute supper. Keep your pantry well stocked to prevent a last-minute rush to a food store. Ingredients in jars or cans will save on preparation time, too—most things can be bought chopped, peeled, or flavored at little or no extra cost. Improvise by using chickpeas when the recipe calls for kidney beans, and for new dishes experiment by using the ingredients buried at the back of the pantry. Most of us have basics, such as pasta, rice, and canned tomatoes, but next time you go shopping, spend some time in the canned food aisle and select a few more unusual ingredients to try.

canned pulses

Most canned pulses are excellent and avoid the lengthy soaking and cooking times needed for dried pulses. Chickpeas can be added to stews and casseroles towards the end of cooking to add substance and a mild, nutty flavor, or nearer the beginning for a richer flavor. Do not stir too much, as they may disintegrate, although they process well to make a smooth soup or sauce. Experiment with adding chickpeas to your usual stuffing recipes. Dried chickpeas take a long time to prepare and there is not a noticeable difference in taste.

Red kidney beans are familiar to most people, usually from the Mexican Chili Con Carne (see page 56), and can be added to any stew or casserole. Drain and rinse before adding to your cooking. They make a substantial meal and add an attractive splash of color. Great Northern beans are best known for their use in tomato sauce as baked beans. Keep a can in the pantry and add to anything from salads to stews. Cannellini beans are white, and have a lovely buttery flavor. They make an interesting addition to casseroles and stews, and cannellini beans processed into a paste can be used to thicken and lighten the color of soups. Flageolet beans are pale green and are not strongly flavored. They are a good choice for children. Their delicate taste will be overpowered in strongly flavored dishes such as curries or stews—try them with salads and with subtly flavored meat dishes.

fish

Canned tuna, salmon, anchovy fillets, and sardines can be valuable pantry stand-bys. You can base a meal around them, or add them to a vegetable dish for extra flavor and color. Use canned tuna in rice dishes, salads, pasta dishes, and potato bakes. Use anchovies sparingly, as they have a strong, very salty flavor. Sardines are rather oily, but are very good for you, and can be served straight from the can with a salad.

flavorings and sauces

Many flavorings used during cooking can also be put in a small dish at the table as a sauce, or drizzled over the dish before serving. Soy sauce is an Asian sauce made from fermented soybeans. Light soy sauce has a saltier, weaker flavor and color than dark soy sauce—it should be used in a dish that requires no extra coloring. Dark soy sauce has a sweeter flavor, and adds an exotic color to vegetable, rice, and noodle dishes, as well as to meat—it should be used for heavy seasoning. No extra salt should be added to dishes with soy sauce in them.

Tabasco sauce is made in Louisiana. It can be added sparingly to soups and casseroles to add moderate heat, or in larger quantities to make very spicy chile dishes. Traditional British sauces such as tomato ketchup, brown sauce, and Worcestershire sauce can add flavor to casseroles. Add liberally to meat dishes.

Chutney is an ideal pantry stand-by. It can be used in obvious ways, such as in cheese sandwiches, but gives a great flavor to casseroles and soups. Try using it as a main ingredient in a stuffing, or add it to a pot roast.

noodles

An Asian alternative to pasta, noodles are healthy, convenient, and quick to cook. They store well and keep for a long time. Use in soups and stir-fries, with sesame oil and soy sauce for the best flavor. Egg noodles are inexpensive and come dried, usually in rectangular cakes. Rice noodles, made from rice flour, are just as easy to cook. Cellophane noodles, also known as transparent, glass, and bean thread noodles, are made from ground mung beans, and must be soaked before use. Most noodles are of medium thickness, although you may find thicker ones in an Asian food store. Long, thin noodles are best for soups and light sauces.

nuts

Most nuts stay fresh for a long time if sealed in an airtight container, although you must use pine nuts relatively quickly, as they have a high fat content and go stale. Try adding pine nuts to salads, stews, ice creams, sundaes, and stuffings. They also make a very attractive garnish. Toast before using, as this improves the flavor. Peanuts can be used to garnish many dishes and are great for a satay sauce to go with whatever meat you have in the freezer. They are also useful as a snack for visitors, but bear in mind that nut allergies are common, and peanut allergies can be particularly dangerous.

oils

There are many different types of oil, but plain corn oil can be used for most purposes. It is more or less flavorless, so can be used in sweet and savory dishes. Olive oil can be very expensive. Buy a lower quality oil— virgin or pure—if you intend to use olive oil for everyday cooking. Extra virgin olive oil is considered to be the best quality, and should be reserved for salad dressings and other dishes in which its flavor is intended to play a part.

For Asian cooking, sesame oil is particularly good. It has a strong taste, so use just a few drops for a stir-fry or in rice or noodle dishes for extra flavor. Use only at moderate temperatures, because it burns easily. It is often added just before serving for extra flavor, rather than used as a cooking oil.

Flavored oils such as herb and garlic oils can be timesaving, because you don't have to chop fresh herbs and garlic separately. To make your own, add a few cloves of garlic and/or a handful of chopped, fresh herbs to a bottle of good-quality oil, seal, and let stand for at least a week to allow the flavors to release and infuse the oil.

olives and capers

Olives are invaluable as a snack, but they can also be incorporated into many dishes. Add them as a garnish or use them as a main ingredient in a dish; try black olives and stuffed green olives, which have different flavors. Both go well with fish, such as canned tuna and salmon. Similarly, capers can add a decorative touch. Add them sparingly to salads, as they have a strong, pickled flavor.

rice

There are many different types of rice. As well as the best known white long- and short-grain rices, you can also buy wild rice, risotto rice, and brown rice. Most dishes can be cooked with more than one type of rice, although some, such as risottos, have to be cooked with a specific type. Black glutinous and wild rice are dark in color; wild rice is actually an aquatic grass. Red rice, such as Wahani from California and the semi-wild Camargue rice, has a pleasant flavor, and can make simple dishes look spectacular. Arborio, carnaroli, and Vialone Nano are all types of round grain risotto rice. They absorb large quantities of liquid and are cooked by a particular method, resulting in the creamy but firm texture unique

to risotto. Brown rice has a nuttier texture than white rice. It takes longer to cook than white rice and will not swell as much, so you will need to use more of it.

tomatoes

Peeled, canned plum tomatoes add flavor, color, and substance to almost any meal, and add bulk to soups and sauces. Chopped sun-dried tomatoes preserved in oil are usually sold in jars and make a great stand-by for sauces and pasta dishes. Add to casseroles and stews for a rich flavor, or to stuffings for color and for a flavor that penetrates the meat. Use the flavored oil as a salad dressing and to cook meats, especially chicken.

Tomato paste is very concentrated and you will need to add only a little to your cooking for a strong flavor and color. Sun-dried tomato paste makes wonderful, flavorsome sauces. It has a darker color than normal tomato paste and a stronger, more particular flavor, so use sparingly at first. If you use tomato paste regularly, buy a jar and store in the refrigerator.

Strained tomatoes are an Italian alternative to canned tomatoes, made from strained and processed tomatoes, and are smoother than canned tomatoes. They are an ideal ingredient for sauces and soups and can be added to casseroles and stews, with delicious results.

vinegars

It is worth experimenting with vinegars other than plain wine vinegar, as they all have unique flavors. You can make your own flavored vinegars using the same method as for flavored oil. Try herb or garlic vinegar—rosemary has a particularly delicious flavor. White wine vinegar can be used for everything from fish and chips to sauces, and is the best choice for salad dressings. Keep tightly sealed to avoid losing any of the flavor. Balsamic vinegar from northern Italy is darker in color than most vinegars. Best used for salad dressings, balsamic vinegar is sometimes aged for up to 20 years, although you should buy a younger, less expensive vinegar for everyday use. Cider vinegar is made from apples and can make a lovely, summery salad dressing. It has a strong, very acidic flavor, and should be used sparingly.

making the most of one-pot dishes

An easy way to make the most of one-pot dishes is to serve them with a side salad of pasta or rice, or more conventional lettuce, cucumber, and tomato. You can change the taste of a whole meal by adding a salad

dressing, either just before you serve, as a garnish, or at the table. Try strongly flavored salad dressings such as blue cheese with meat dishes, and lighter dressings such as vinaigrette with chicken and risottos.

Experiment with adding more unusual ingredients to salads, such as fruit, nuts, croutons, or lardons. Segments of orange add a lovely tangy flavor, as well as a splash of color. Try adding fruit to a salad when serving with meat that traditionally goes well with fruit, such as duck or pork. Pine nuts, especially if they are toasted, make a quick and attractive addition and will not overwhelm the flavor of anything else. Croutons are often flavored with garlic and/or herbs and are best added to a salad served with a strongly flavored dish. Add them just before serving, otherwise they tend to go soggy. If croutons in your pantry go stale, sprinkle them with a little milk, spread out on a cookie sheet, and bake in a preheated oven, 425°F/220°C, for a few minutes, until crispy again—serve immediately. Ready-made lardons and croutons are available in most major food stores, and will retain their flavor and crispness as long as they are stored adequately.

Nowadays, many unusual and exotic types of salad greens are available. Experiment with their different flavors, colors, and textures. Try salads made with arugula, oak leaf, radicchio, mizuna, and tatsoi, or combine these with more conventional greens, such as romaine, Boston, and iceberg lettuces, and more conventional ingredients, such as tomatoes, radishes, and beets for color, and scallions, shredded cabbage, and anchovies for flavor. Baby spinach leaves also make good salads. Look at your pantry stand-bys for inspiration—try adding tuna, capers, a drizzle of balsamic vinegar, and/or freshly grated Parmesan cheese.

Fresh herbs are a simple and attractive addition to salads. Try adding dill to a potato salad or a salad served with fish. A drizzle of olive oil and a handful of fresh, chopped herbs are all that is needed for many salads—chives are an excellent addition.

You can make your own salads of delicatessen quality at home, as well as plain lettuce and tomato salads. Pasta salad and rice salad can be made as a one-pot dish. Add any fresh vegetables that you have in the refrigerator—bell peppers, diced cucumber, bean sprouts, grated carrot—and you can also add hard-cooked eggs, peanuts, sunflower seeds, or cubes of cheese. You can make it up as you go along, and this can be one of the most enjoyable ways of preparing a meal. You can use potatoes and pulses as a main ingredient, too. Mixed bean salad is delicious made with red kidney beans, cannellini beans, and Great Northern beans, and is quick and easy to make. You can base your salad around any ingredients; try tomato salad with onions, or coleslaw with sultanas.

Many salad dressings can easily be made at home and will keep quite well in the refrigerator. Their flavor will be superior to store-bought versions, and you can eliminate the need for colorings, additives, and preservatives. You can add a handful of chopped fresh herbs or other ingredients to a plain mayonnaise to adapt it to the dish you are serving. Try adding a handful of crumbled blue cheese, such as Stilton, to a plain mayonnaise and beat well, to make a strong and delicious accompaniment to stews and casseroles. Add freshly snipped chives or dill for a salad dressing, which will complement chicken, potatoes, or fish. You can add anything—try sun-dried tomato or garlic oil in a dressing in place of the plain oil.

Bread is also a great accompaniment to most one-pot dishes, and can be served with or instead of a salad. Slices of basic white bread can be used for mopping up juices from stews, soups, and casseroles, but many different and more interesting breads are now available. Most freeze well, and will keep for up to three months in the freezer. Remove and let stand at room temperature for about 24 hours before serving.

Most major food stores and some smaller stores now have quite an extensive range of French bread, Italian bread, and other more exotic breads. French bread is delicious served with soups, is inexpensive, and looks attractive. Serve fresh and warm, if possible, with lots of butter and a side salad. Ciabatta and focaccia are Italian breads, most often baked with herbs. Both of these are ideal for serving with or at the end of a meal with lots of sauce, especially soups and stews. Improvise with the bread that is available in the shops, or bake it at home. Freeze a few different types of bread if your local food store has a good selection.

You can make an easy cheat's garlic bread by buying hot, fresh French bread if you live near a bakery. Make some garlic butter using soft, warm butter, a little garlic, herbs, and salt and pepper. Make vertical slits along the length of the bread with a sharp knife, then spread a little of the garlic butter inside the slits. Make sure the bread and butter are warm and that you use only a little garlic—it will taste stronger because it has not been cooked.

A simple way to liven up stews and casseroles and make them into a more substantial meal is to top them with bread and cheese. French bread works well, but you can use any bread that can be cut into thick slices. This is a great way to use up stale bread, as it works better than fresh bread. Cut the loaf into thick slices and spread with a thin layer of butter or olive oil. Thinly slice some cheese—Cheddar, Edam, and Swiss cheese work well—and place some on top of each slice of bread. Towards the end of cooking, place the slices of bread and cheese on top of the casserole so that the bottom of the bread absorbs a little of the sauce and the cheese melts. Depending on your tastes, you may like to try placing a slice of tomato between the bread and cheese before cooking. If you are going to use oil instead of butter, a spray canister of oil ensures that you do not use too much. Alternatively, you could place a slice of bread and cheese in the bottom of each individual soup bowl before ladling in hot soup.

If you are making a one-pot soup and it looks too weak, try adding pâté to thicken it and add flavor. This works best with strongly flavored soups, such as tomato, beef, and lentil.

To add an attractive garnish to bowls of tomato soup and other dark-colored soups, place a small spoonful of cream in the center and run a toothpick through it to make a swirl. Sour cream or ricotta cheese add a creamy texture and flavor to soups, and should be added towards the end of cooking to heat through.

desserts

Most one-pot desserts are a complete dish and don't need anything added. However, if you have a large family or a very hungry one, you may want to pad out the dish. The easiest thing to add to desserts is canned fruit—try a pineapple ring on top of each portion, or serve with a separate fruit salad. Try using canned mandarin segments, grapefruit, or lychees, which go well with ice cream. Fresh

fruit takes a little more preparation, and you have to bear in mind the time of year—will you be able to get fresh strawberries or blueberries?

Plain yogurt can be added to many desserts with a small bowl of sugar, honey, or syrup at the table. Intensely flavored honeys, such as orange blossom, are particularly delicious and are often attractive colors. Fruit-flavored yogurts are cheap and quick, and can be added by the spoonful to the dessert or served separately in a bowl at the table.

Light cream is a classic with strawberries, raspberries, and other fresh fruits, but for most other desserts, heavy cream or whipped cream is best. You can buy whipped cream in a spray form, saving time and effort, but this is not nearly as flavorsome or pleasant in texture as freshly whipped heavy cream. Mascarpone is an alternative to cream—it is deliciously thick and creamy, and you will probably need only a small tub.

If you have a sweet tooth, try adding syrups or jellies to your desserts. If you use a canned fruit for a dessert, reserve the syrup from the can to serve with another dessert the following day. Apricot jelly goes well with pastries and pies, while black currant and blueberry jellies are delicious with baked dishes, such as muffins or biscuits. Dessert sauce can be bought in many flavors, such as chocolate, caramel, strawberry, and raspberry, and is usually very sweet. Use as an alternative to syrups and jellies when you run out—it keeps for a long time.

Grate chocolate over a dish while it is still warm—much easier than melting chocolate in a bowl set over a pan of hot water. Grated chocolate is also delicious sprinkled over ice cream or cream and fresh fruit.

Ice cream and flavored gelatin desserts are traditional children's favorites, but need not be limited to the little ones. Make adult gelatin desserts by adding a little alcohol and fruit and serve at an evening meal. To make a children's version more interesting, add some edible treats at the bottom of the mold before letting them set, though these are not suitable for children under three.

basic recipes

mayonnaise

makes: generous ¾ cup
preparation time: 15 minutes

1 egg
3 garlic cloves (optional)
⅔ cup flavored or plain oil
½ tsp cider vinegar
pinch of paprika
salt and pepper

1 Break the egg into a blender or food processor and add the garlic (if using). Process for 30 seconds.

2 Add a little oil, process, add a little more, and process. Continue adding until it is all incorporated and the mixture is thick, creamy, and pale yellow.

3 Pour the mayonnaise into a bowl and gradually beat in the vinegar. Season with the paprika, salt, and pepper.

vegetable stock

makes: about 8 cups
preparation time: 10 minutes
cooking time: 35 minutes

2 tbsp corn oil
4 oz/115 g onions, finely chopped
4 oz/115 g leeks, finely chopped
4 oz/115 g carrots, finely chopped
4 celery stalks, finely chopped
3 oz/85 g fennel, finely chopped
3 oz/85 g tomatoes, finely chopped
9¼ cups water
1 bouquet garni

1 Heat the oil in a pan. Add the onions and leeks and cook over low heat for 5 minutes, or until softened.

2 Add the remaining vegetables, cover, and cook for 10 minutes. Add the water and bouquet garni, bring to a boil, and simmer for 20 minutes.

3 Strain, cool, and store in the refrigerator. Use immediately or freeze in portions for up to 3 months.

fish stock

makes: 5½ cups
preparation time: 10 minutes
cooking time: 30 minutes

1 lb 7 oz/650 g white fish heads, bones, and trimmings, rinsed
1 onion, sliced
2 celery stalks, chopped
1 carrot, sliced
1 bay leaf
4 fresh parsley sprigs
4 black peppercorns
½ lemon, sliced
5½ cups water
½ cup dry white wine

1 Place the fish heads, bones, and trimmings in a large pan. Add all of the remaining ingredients and bring to a boil, skimming off the foam that rises to the surface.

2 Reduce the heat, partially cover, and simmer gently for 25 minutes.

3 Strain the stock, without pressing down on the contents of the strainer. Cool and store in the refrigerator. Use immediately or freeze in portions for up to 3 months.

chicken stock

makes: scant 10 cups
preparation time: 10 minutes
cooking time: 3½ hours

3 lb/1.3 kg chicken wings and necks
2 onions, cut into wedges
16 cups water
2 carrots, coarsely chopped
2 celery stalks, coarsely chopped
10 fresh parsley sprigs
4 fresh thyme sprigs
2 bay leaves
10 black peppercorns

1 Place the chicken wings and necks and the onions in a large, heavy-bottomed pan and cook over low heat, stirring frequently, until lightly browned.

2 Add the water and stir thoroughly to scrape off any sediment on the bottom of the pan. Bring to a boil, skimming off any foam that rises to the surface. Add all of the remaining ingredients, partially cover, and simmer gently for 3 hours.

3 Strain, cool, and place in the refrigerator. When cold, carefully remove and discard the layer of fat on the surface. Use immediately or freeze in portions for up to 6 months.

beef stock

makes: about 7 cups
preparation time: 10 minutes
cooking time: 4½ hours

2 lb 4 oz/1 kg beef marrow bones, sawn into 3-inch/7.5-cm pieces
1 lb 7 oz/650 g stewing beef in 1 piece
11 cups water
4 cloves
2 onions, halved
2 celery stalks, coarsely chopped
8 peppercorns
1 bouquet garni

1 Place the beef marrow bones in a heavy-bottomed pan and put the stewing beef on top. Add the water and bring to a boil over low heat, skimming off any foam that rises to the surface.

2 Press a clove into each onion half and add to the pan with the celery, peppercorns, and bouquet garni. Partially cover and simmer very gently for 3 hours. Remove the meat and simmer for 1 hour.

3 Strain, cool, and place in the refrigerator. When cold, carefully remove and discard the layer of fat on the surface. Use immediately or freeze in portions for up to 6 months.

soups

There is something especially appetizing about home-made soup, whether it is chunky and hearty, such as Bacon & Lentil Soup (see page 21), or delicate and fragrant, such as Avgolemono (see page 49). Most of the soups in this chapter make a good start to a meal or, served with some fresh rolls or crusty bread, a light lunch or evening snack.

It is worth making your own stock (see page 13)—and that's only one pot, too— because that way, you can be sure of the quality and flavor. Chicken stock is a good all-round ingredient, if you don't want to bother making several different types of stock, and it can even be used for fish soups. If you do have to use stock cubes, look for ones with a low salt content and be careful when you season the soup.

The recipes incorporate all kinds of ingredients: an entire chicken supplies both the broth and the meat for two separate dishes in the classic Scottish Cock-a-Leekie (see page 23) and a veritable market garden of vegetables is found in Italian Minestrone (see page 33). There are spicy soups from Asia, hearty country soups from France, and fabulous fish soups from both America and the Mediterranean. There are familiar family favorites, such as Chicken Soup (see page 22), and some more unusual ideas, such as Corn, Potato & Cheese Soup (see page 45). All are easy to make and some are surprisingly quick, so you are sure to find one to please you and your family.

cabbage soup with sausage

cook: 1 hr 15 mins   **prep: 15 mins**   **serves 6**

NUTRITIONAL INFORMATION

Calories	246
Protein	. . . . .15g
Carbohydrate	. . . . .21g
Sugars	. . . . .13g
Fat	. . . . .12g
Saturates	. . . . .4g

variation

If you wish, substitute any other meat stock, such as Beef Stock (see page 13), for the Chicken Stock in this soup.

Spicy or smoky sausages add substance to this soup, which makes a hearty and warming supper served with crusty bread and salad greens.

INGREDIENTS

12 oz/350 g lean sausages, preferably highly seasoned

2 tsp olive oil

1 onion, finely chopped

1 leek, halved lengthwise and thinly sliced

2 carrots, halved and thinly sliced

14 oz/400 g canned chopped tomatoes

12 oz/350 g young green cabbage, cored and coarsely shredded

1–2 garlic cloves, finely chopped

pinch of dried thyme

6½ cups Chicken Stock (see page 13)

salt and pepper

freshly grated Parmesan cheese, to serve

cook's tip

If you don't have fresh stock, use water with 1 stock cube dissolved in it. Add a little more onion and garlic, plus a bouquet garni (remove it before serving).

1 Place the sausages in a large pan, pour in enough water to cover generously, and bring to a boil. Reduce the heat and simmer until firm. Drain the sausages and, when cool enough to handle, remove the skin, if you like. Slice thinly.

2 Heat the olive oil in a separate large pan.

Add the onion, leek, and carrots and cook over medium heat for 3–4 minutes, stirring constantly, until the onion begins to soften.

3 Add the tomatoes, cabbage, garlic, thyme, Stock, and sausages. Season to taste with salt and pepper. Bring to a boil, reduce the heat to low, and cook gently,

partially covered, for 40 minutes, or until the vegetables are tender.

4 Taste the soup and adjust the seasoning, if necessary. Ladle into warmed bowls and serve with the grated Parmesan cheese.

frankfurter & field pea broth

serves 6   **prep: 15 mins** ⏱   **cook: 2 hrs 30 mins** ⏱

*Economical, nourishing, filling, and packed with flavor—
what more could you ask for on a cold evening?*

INGREDIENTS

8 oz/225 g salt belly of pork,
cut into cubes

scant 10 cups water

1 lb 2 oz/500 g field peas, soaked in
enough cold water to cover for 2 hours

4 onions, chopped

2 leeks, chopped

4 carrots, chopped

4 celery stalks, chopped

1 cooking apple, peeled,
cored, and chopped

1 tbsp brown sugar

1 bouquet garni

6 frankfurters, cut into
1-inch/2.5-cm lengths

2 tbsp butter

salt and pepper

celery leaves, to garnish

variation

Substitute other favorite vegetables,
such as parsnips and bell peppers, for
the carrots and celery, if you prefer.

cook's tip

You can use yellow or green
split peas for this soup. The
cooking time may vary
depending on their freshness
—the fresher they are, the
quicker they will cook.

1 Put the pork cubes into a large, heavy-bottomed pan and add enough cold water to cover. Bring to a boil over low heat, then drain well. Return the pork to the pan and add the water.

2 Drain and rinse the peas, then add them to the pan with the onions, leeks, carrots, celery, apple, sugar, and bouquet garni. Bring to a boil, skimming off any scum that rises to the surface. Reduce the heat, cover, and simmer, stirring occasionally, for 2 hours.

3 Remove and discard the bouquet garni and stir in the frankfurters and butter. Season to taste with salt and pepper and heat through. Ladle into warmed bowls, garnish with celery leaves, and serve immediately.

bacon & lentil soup

⏱ **cook: 1 hr 15 mins**　　　⏲ **prep: 15 mins**　　　　**serves 4**

NUTRITIONAL INFORMATION	
Calories	.612
Protein	.23g
Carbohydrate	.26g
Sugars	7g
Fat	.47g
Saturates	.18g

variation

You can use different root vegetables, such as swede and parsnips, instead of the carrots and turnips, if you prefer.

Bacon and lentils have a real affinity—their flavors and textures complement one another. This popular family supper also includes a wide selection of tasty vegetables.

INGREDIENTS

1 lb/450 g thick, rindless smoked bacon strips, diced
1 onion, chopped
2 carrots, sliced
2 celery stalks, chopped
1 turnip, chopped
1 large potato, chopped
generous 2¼ cups Puy lentils
1 bouquet garni
4 cups water or Chicken Stock (see page 13)
salt and pepper

cook's tip

Do not add any salt until the lentils have finished cooking, otherwise they will toughen, which will impair the texture of the soup.

1 Heat a large, heavy-bottomed pan or flameproof casserole. Add the bacon and cook over medium heat, stirring, for 4–5 minutes, or until the fat runs. Add the chopped onion, carrots, celery, turnip, and potato and cook, stirring frequently, for 5 minutes.

2 Add the lentils and bouquet garni and pour in the water. Bring to a boil, reduce the heat, and simmer for 1 hour, or until the lentils are tender.

3 Remove and discard the bouquet garni and season the soup to taste with pepper, and with salt if necessary. Ladle into warmed soup bowls and serve.

chicken soup

serves 4 | **prep: 10 mins** | **cook: 30 mins**

A farmhouse classic, this delicious, hearty soup is packed with flavor, and makes a comforting one-pot meal. Serve with a generous side order of fresh, crusty bread.

INGREDIENTS

2 tbsp butter

1 small onion, finely chopped

1 leek, thinly sliced

4 skinless, boneless chicken thighs, diced

⅛ cup long-grain rice

scant 3½ cups Chicken Stock (see page 13)

1 tbsp chopped fresh parsley

salt and pepper

fresh parsley sprigs, to garnish

NUTRITIONAL INFORMATION	
Calories 136
Protein 10g
Carbohydrate 7g
Sugars 1g
Fat 8g
Saturates 4g

cook's tip

You can add other vegetables, such as diced carrot, with the onion and leeks in Step 1, or fresh beans or peas just before pouring in the Stock in Step 2.

1 Melt the butter in a large, heavy-bottomed pan. Add the onion and leek and cook over low heat, stirring occasionally, for 5 minutes, or until softened. Add the chicken and cook over medium heat for 2 minutes.

2 Add the rice and cook, stirring constantly, for 1 minute, or until the grains are coated with butter. Pour in the Stock, bring to a boil, reduce the heat, and simmer for 20 minutes, or until the chicken and rice are tender.

3 Stir in the parsley and season the soup to taste with salt and pepper. Ladle into warmed bowls, garnish with parsley sprigs, and serve immediately.

cock-a-leekie

cook: 2 hrs 45 mins   **prep: 15 mins**   **serves 6**

Two for the price of one—serve the soup separately as an appetizer and the meat and vegetables as a main meal. Alternatively, for a really chunky dish, ladle the whole thing into large soup plates.

NUTRITIONAL INFORMATION	
Calories	348
Protein	21g
Carbohydrate	29g
Sugars	28g
Fat	18g
Saturates	6g

INGREDIENTS

3 lb/1.3 kg chicken

9¼ cups Beef Stock (see page 13)

2 lb/900 g leeks

1 bouquet garni

salt and pepper

1 lb/450 g prunes, pitted and
soaked overnight in enough
cold water to cover

cook's tip

A bouquet garni usually consists of 3 fresh parsley sprigs, 2 fresh thyme sprigs, and a bay leaf, tied together in a bundle.

1 Put the chicken, breast-side down, in a large, heavy-bottomed pan or flameproof casserole. Pour in the Stock and bring to a boil, skimming off any scum that rises to the surface.

2 Tie half the leeks together in a bundle with kitchen string and thinly slice the remainder. Add the bundle of leeks to the pan with the bouquet garni and a pinch of salt, reduce the heat, partially cover, and simmer for 2 hours, or until the chicken is tender.

3 Remove and discard the bundle of leeks and bouquet garni. Drain the prunes, add them to the pan, and simmer for 20 minutes. Season to taste with salt and pepper and add the sliced leeks. Simmer for an additional 10 minutes. Slice the chicken, or cut into bite-size pieces, and serve.

beef & vegetable soup

serves 6   **prep: 20 mins** ⏲   **cook: 25 mins** ⏲

This colorful, spicy soup comes from South-east Asia, where it would be served with plain boiled rice, but it is substantial enough to make a filling meal on its own.

INGREDIENTS

2 tbsp peanut or corn oil	4 cups Chicken or Beef Stock
1 large onion, finely chopped	(see page 13)
4 oz/115 g fresh lean ground beef	salt
1 garlic clove, finely chopped	4 oz/115 g cooked peeled shrimp
2 fresh red chiles, seeded and	8 oz/225 g fresh spinach, coarse stems
finely chopped	removed and leaves shredded
1 tbsp ground almonds	6 oz/175 g baby corn cobs, sliced
1 carrot, grated	1 beefsteak tomato, chopped
1 tsp brown sugar	2 tbsp lime juice
½-inch/1-cm cube shrimp	
paste (optional)	

NUTRITIONAL INFORMATION

Calories	140
Protein	12g
Carbohydrate	8g
Sugars	6g
Fat	7g
Saturates	1g

variation

Replace the cooked shrimp with 2 oz/ 55 g of dried shrimp soaked in hot water for 10 minutes. Add the shrimp and soaking water in Step 2.

cook's tip

Shrimp paste, also known as blachan and terasi, is available from Chinese food stores. Before use, wrap a cube of it in foil and place in a skillet over low heat, turning occasionally, for 5 minutes.

1 Heat the oil in a large, heavy-bottomed pan. Add the onion and cook over low heat, stirring occasionally, for 5 minutes, or until softened. Add the beef and garlic and cook, stirring, until the meat is browned.

2 Add the chiles, ground almonds, grated carrot, and sugar. Add the shrimp paste (if using). Pour in the Stock and season to taste with salt. Bring the mixture to a boil over low heat, then simmer for 10 minutes.

3 Stir in the shrimp, spinach, corn cobs, tomato, and lime juice. Simmer the mixture for an additional 2–3 minutes, or until heated through. Ladle into warmed bowls and serve.

scotch broth

cook: 1 hr 30 mins   **prep: 10–15 mins**   **serves 4**

NUTRITIONAL INFORMATION

Calories 186

Protein 13g

Carbohydrate 23g

Sugars 6g

Fat 5g

Saturates 2g

variation

Replace the rutabaga with the same amount of turnip and substitute the parsnip with potato, if you prefer.

This traditional, warming soup is full of goodness, with lots of tasty golden vegetables along with tender barley and lamb.

INGREDIENTS

¼ cup pearl barley	1 bay leaf
10½ oz/300 g lean, boneless lamb, such	1 large leek, cut into fourths
as shoulder or neck fillet, trimmed of	lengthwise and sliced
fat and cut into ½-inch/1-cm cubes	2 large carrots, finely diced
scant 3 cups water	1 parsnip, finely diced
2 garlic cloves, finely chopped	4½ oz/125 g rutabaga, diced
or crushed	salt and pepper
4 cups Chicken Stock	2 tbsp chopped fresh parsley
(see page 13)	fresh parsley sprigs, to garnish
1 onion, finely chopped	crusty bread, to serve

cook's tip

This soup is lean when the lamb is trimmed. By making it beforehand and chilling in the refrigerator, you can remove any hardened fat before reheating it.

1 Rinse the barley under cold running water. Place in a large, heavy-bottomed pan and pour in enough water to cover. Bring to a boil over medium heat and boil for 3 minutes, skimming off any foam that rises to the surface. Remove the pan from the heat, cover, and reserve until required.

2 Place the lamb in a separate large, heavy-bottomed pan with the water and bring to a boil. Skim off any foam that rises to the surface. Stir in the garlic, Stock, onion, and bay leaf. Reduce the heat, partially cover, and simmer for 15 minutes.

3 Drain the barley and add to the soup.

Add the leek, carrots, parsnip, and rutabaga. Simmer, stirring occasionally, for 1 hour, or until the lamb and vegetables are cooked.

4 Season to taste with salt and pepper and stir in the chopped parsley. Ladle into warmed serving bowls, garnish with parsley sprigs, and serve with crusty bread.

quick clam chowder

 cook: 35 mins   prep: 10 mins   serves 4

NUTRITIONAL INFORMATION

Calories 356

Protein 24g

Carbohydrate 23g

Sugars 7g

Fat 19g

Saturates 8g

variation

If you like, add 1–2 fresh red chiles, seeded and sliced, to the pan in Step 2 and continue as in the main recipe.

There are many versions of this classic, rich shellfish soup. New England chowder uses milk rather than stock and has no tomatoes. This is a version of Manhattan clam chowder.

INGREDIENTS

2 tsp corn oil

4 oz/115 g rindless lean bacon, diced

2 tbsp butter

1 onion, chopped

2 celery stalks, chopped

2 potatoes, chopped

salt and pepper

2 leeks, sliced

14 oz/400 g canned chopped tomatoes

3 tbsp chopped fresh parsley

5 cups Fish Stock (see page 13)

1 lb 4 oz/550 g canned clams, drained and rinsed

cook's tip

Canned clams are available all year round from most major food stores. They take the effort out of preparing clam chowder, and make a quick, easy, and unusual soup.

1 Heat the oil in a heavy-bottomed pan. Add the bacon and cook over medium heat, stirring, for 5 minutes, or until the fat runs and it begins to crisp. Remove from the pan, drain on paper towels, and reserve.

2 Add the butter to the pan and stir to melt. Add the onion, celery, and potatoes with a pinch of salt. Cover and cook over low heat, stirring occasionally, for 10 minutes, or until soft.

3 Stir in the leeks, the tomatoes and their juices, and 2 tablespoons of the parsley. Pour in the Stock, bring to a boil, reduce the heat, and simmer for 10–15 minutes, or until the vegetables are tender. Season to taste with salt and pepper and stir in the clams. Heat the soup through gently for 2–3 minutes, then ladle into warmed bowls, garnish with the remaining parsley and reserved bacon, and serve.

genoese fish soup

serves 4 **prep: 15 mins** ⟲ **cook: 25 mins** ⟳

You can use any firm white fish fillets for this tasty soup. The best way to remove any small bones is to pull them out with tweezers before you begin chopping the flesh.

INGREDIENTS

2 tbsp butter

1 onion, chopped

1 garlic clove, finely chopped

2 oz/55 g rindless lean bacon, diced

2 celery stalks, chopped

14 oz/400 g canned chopped tomatoes

⅔ cup dry white wine

1¼ cups Fish Stock (see page 13)

4 fresh basil leaves, torn

2 tbsp chopped fresh flatleaf parsley

salt and pepper

1 lb/450 g white fish fillets, such as cod or angler fish, skinned and chopped

4 oz/115 g cooked peeled shrimp

NUTRITIONAL INFORMATION	
Calories	276
Protein	30g
Carbohydrate	7g
Sugars	5g
Fat	12g
Saturates	6g

variation

You could also use haddock, ling, or sea bass to make this dish. If you are on a budget, coley would make a cheaper alternative.

cook's tip

Angler fish is a good choice for this soup, as it has only a single central bone down the tail. Make sure you peel off the gray membrane from the flesh before chopping and cooking.

  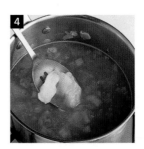

1 Melt the butter in a large, heavy-bottomed pan. Add the chopped onion and garlic and cook over low heat, stirring occasionally, for 5 minutes, or until softened.

2 Add the lean bacon and celery and cook, stirring frequently, for an additional 2 minutes.

3 Add the tomatoes and their juices, the wine, Stock, basil, and 1 tablespoon of the parsley. Season to taste with salt and pepper. Bring to a boil, then reduce the heat and simmer for 10 minutes.

4 Add the fish and cook for 5 minutes, or until it is opaque. Add the shrimp and heat through gently for 3 minutes. Ladle into a warmed tureen, garnish with the remaining parsley, and serve immediately.

minestrone

⏱ **cook: 1 hr 30 mins–2 hrs**   ⏱ **prep: 15 mins**   **serves 4**

NUTRITIONAL INFORMATION	
Calories 440	
Protein 18g	
Carbohydrate 67g	
Sugars 16g	
Fat 13g	
Saturates 3g	

variation

Although the Great Northern beans are a traditional ingredient for this soup, you could substitute cannellini or pinto beans, if you prefer.

Ever-popular, this fabulous Italian soup contains a cornucopia of fresh and dried vegetables—virtually every Italian cook has their own personal version of the recipe.

INGREDIENTS

3 tbsp olive oil

2 onions, chopped

½ small green or savoy cabbage, thick stems removed and leaves shredded

2 zucchini, chopped

2 celery stalks, chopped

2 carrots, chopped

2 potatoes, chopped

4 large tomatoes, peeled and chopped

4 oz/115 g dried Great Northern beans, soaked overnight in enough cold water to cover

5 cups Chicken or Vegetable Stock (see page 13)

4 oz/115 g dried soup pasta

salt and pepper

freshly shaved Parmesan cheese, to garnish

4 tbsp freshly grated Parmesan cheese, to serve

cook's tip

It is not absolutely necessary to use a flavored stock for this soup. If you want to make minestrone without making stock, just substitute the same amount of water.

1 Heat the oil in a large heavy-bottomed pan. Add the onions and cook over low heat, stirring occasionally, for 5 minutes, or until softened.

2 Add the cabbage, zucchini, celery, carrots, potatoes, and tomatoes to the pan, cover, and cook, stirring occasionally, for 10 minutes.

3 Drain and rinse the beans, then add to the pan. Pour in the Stock, bring to a boil, cover, and simmer for 1–1½ hours, or until the beans are tender.

4 Add the soup pasta to the pan and cook, uncovered, for 8–10 minutes, or until tender but still firm to the bite. Season to taste with salt and pepper and ladle into warmed bowls. Garnish with fresh Parmesan cheese shavings and an extra sprinkling of pepper. Serve, handing the grated Parmesan cheese separately.

indian potato & pea soup

serves 4 **prep: 5 mins** 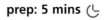 **cook: 35 mins**

A slightly hot and spicy Indian flavor is given to this soup with the use of garam masala, chile, cumin, and ground coriander—ideal for warming up a cold evening.

INGREDIENTS

2 tbsp vegetable oil

8 oz/225 g floury potatoes, diced

1 large onion, chopped

2 garlic cloves, crushed

1 tsp garam masala

1 tsp ground coriander

1 tsp ground cumin

scant 3½ cups Vegetable Stock (see page 13)

1 fresh red chile, seeded and chopped

1 cup frozen peas

4 tbsp plain yogurt

salt and pepper

chopped fresh cilantro, to garnish

NUTRITIONAL INFORMATION

Calories	153
Protein	6g
Carbohydrate	18g
Sugars	6g
Fat	6g
Saturates	1g

cook's tip

Always wash your hands after handling chiles, because they contain volatile oils that can irritate the skin and make your eyes and lips burn if you touch your face after chopping them.

1 Heat the vegetable oil in a large, heavy-bottomed pan. Add the potatoes, onion, and garlic and cook over low heat, stirring constantly, for 5 minutes.

2 Add the garam masala, ground coriander, and cumin and cook, stirring constantly, for 1 minute, then stir in the Vegetable Stock and chile and bring the mixture to a boil. Reduce the heat, cover, and simmer for 20 minutes, or until the potatoes begin to break down.

3 Add the peas and cook for an additional 5 minutes. Stir in the yogurt and season to taste with salt and pepper. Ladle into warmed soup bowls, garnish with chopped fresh cilantro and serve.

mushroom & gingerroot soup

cook: 15 mins

prep: 10 mins, plus 30 mins soaking (optional)

serves 4

Thai soups are very quickly and easily put together, and are cooked so that each ingredient can still be tasted in the finished dish. The noodles make the soup into a meal in itself.

NUTRITIONAL INFORMATION	
Calories	.74
Protein	.3g
Carbohydrate	.9g
Sugars	.1g
Fat	.3g
Saturates	.0.4g

INGREDIENTS

½ oz/15 g dried Chinese mushrooms or 4½ oz/125 g portobello or cremini mushrooms

4 cups hot Vegetable Stock (see page 13)

4½ oz/125 g thread egg noodles

2 tsp corn oil

3 garlic cloves, crushed

1-inch/2.5-cm piece fresh gingerroot, finely shredded

½ tsp mushroom ketchup

1 tsp light soy sauce

4½ oz/125 g bean sprouts

fresh cilantro sprigs, to garnish

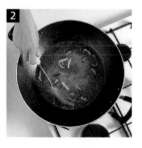

cook's tip

If you are on a lowfat diet, substitute rice noodles for the egg noodles. They contain no fat, and are an ideal way to bulk out a thin soup.

1 Soak the dried Chinese mushrooms (if using) for at least 30 minutes in 1¼ cups of the hot Stock. Drain the mushrooms and reserve the Stock. Remove the stems of the mushrooms and discard. Slice the caps and reserve. Cook the noodles for 2–3 minutes in boiling water, then drain and rinse. Reserve until required.

2 Heat the corn oil in a preheated wok or large, heavy-bottomed skillet over high heat. Add the garlic and gingerroot, stir, and add the mushrooms. Stir over high heat for 2 minutes.

3 Add the remaining Vegetable Stock with the reserved mushroom Stock and bring to a boil. Add the mushroom ketchup and soy sauce. Stir in the bean sprouts and cook until tender. Place some noodles in each soup bowl and ladle the soup on top. Garnish with fresh cilantro sprigs and serve immediately.

green vegetable soup

serves 6 | **prep: 20 mins** ⏲ | **cook: 50 mins** ⏲

This soup takes advantage of a medley of summer vegetables bursting with seasonal flavor. For the best results, use the freshest produce you can find.

INGREDIENTS

1 tbsp olive oil

1 onion, finely chopped

1 large leek, split and thinly sliced

1 celery stalk, thinly sliced

1 carrot, cut into fourths and thinly sliced

1 garlic clove, finely chopped

6¼ cups water

1 potato, diced

1 parsnip, finely diced

1 small kohlrabi, diced

5½ oz/150 g French beans, cut into small pieces

1½ cups fresh or frozen peas

14 oz/400 g canned flageolet beans, drained and rinsed

2 small zucchini, cut into fourths lengthwise and sliced

salt and pepper

3½ oz/100 g spinach leaves, shredded

PESTO

1 large garlic clove, finely chopped

½ oz/15 g fresh basil leaves

4 tbsp extra virgin olive oil

generous ¾ cup freshly grated Parmesan cheese

NUTRITIONAL INFORMATION	
Calories	.260
Protein	.12g
Carbohydrate	.21g
Sugars	.7g
Fat	.15g
Saturates	.4g

variation

If you cannot find a kohlrabi to use in this soup, substitute diced turnip where the kohlrabi is added in Step 2.

cook's tip

You do not have to use a blender or food processor to make pesto. Grinding the ingredients together with a pestle and mortar will work just as well.

1 Heat the oil in a large, heavy-bottomed pan. Add the onion and leek and cook over low heat, stirring occasionally, for 5 minutes. Add the celery, carrot, and garlic, cover, and cook for an additional 5 minutes.

2 Add the water, potato, parsnip, kohlrabi, and French beans. Bring to a boil, reduce the heat, cover, and simmer for 5 minutes. Add the peas, flageolet beans, and zucchini, and season to taste with salt and pepper. Cover and simmer for 25 minutes, or until the vegetables are tender.

3 Meanwhile, make the pesto. Place all of the ingredients in a blender or food processor, reserving a few basil leaves for the garnish. Process until smooth, then reserve until required.

4 Add the spinach to the soup and simmer for 5 minutes. Stir in a spoonful of the pesto. Ladle the soup into warmed soup bowls, garnish with the reserved basil leaves, and serve the remaining pesto separately.

hot & sour soup

cook: 10 mins

prep: 10 mins, plus 20 mins soaking

serves 6

In a typically Chinese approach, the flavors of this spicy Eastern soup are perfectly balanced, and are brought together in a harmonious blend of complementary colors and textures.

INGREDIENTS

6 dried Chinese mushrooms

½ oz/15 g cloud ears (see Cook's Tip)

6¼ cups Chicken Stock (see page 13)

4 tbsp rice wine vinegar

2 tsp chili sauce

1 tbsp dark soy sauce

1 tbsp Chinese rice wine

1 garlic clove, finely chopped

2 tsp finely chopped fresh gingerroot

1 carrot, cut into thin strips

6 oz/175 g canned bamboo shoots, drained, rinsed, and cut into thin strips

8 oz/225 g firm bean curd (drained weight)

2 tbsp cornstarch

3 tbsp water

4 scallions, thinly sliced diagonally, to garnish

variation

If you cannot find any Chinese rice wine for this soup, substitute dry sherry, which works almost as well.

cook's tip

Cloud ears, Chinese fungi that grow on trees, are available from Chinese food stores. They are used in soup, more for texture than flavor. The similar wood ears feature in stir-fries and fish dishes.

1 Place the mushrooms and cloud ears in separate bowls, then add enough boiling water to each bowl to cover. Let soak for 20 minutes. Drain the mushrooms, then remove and discard the stems and thinly slice the caps. Drain and rinse the cloud ears, then cut off any woody parts and thinly slice.

2 Heat the Stock in a large pan. Add the mushrooms, cloud ears, vinegar, chili sauce, soy sauce, Chinese rice wine, garlic, gingerroot, carrot, and bamboo shoots. Bring the mixture to a boil.

3 Meanwhile, cut the bean curd into thin slices and reserve. Combine the cornstarch and water to make a smooth paste. Stir the paste into the boiling soup, reduce the heat, and simmer, stirring constantly, for 3 minutes, or until slightly thickened. Stir in the bean curd and heat through. Ladle the soup into warmed bowls, garnish with the scallions, and serve immediately.

mulligatawny soup

serves 4   **prep: 20 mins** ⟲   **cook: 1 hr 45 mins–2 hrs** ⟳

Redolent of the days of the British Raj, this spicy soup was imported by colonials returning home from India. The sun has long since set on the Empire, but this "pepper water" remains a perennial favorite.

INGREDIENTS

4 tbsp peanut or corn oil

2 chicken pieces, about 12 oz/350 g each

1 onion, chopped

1 carrot, chopped

1 turnip, chopped

1 tbsp curry paste

8 black peppercorns, crushed

4 cloves

¼ cup red split lentils

scant 3½ cups Chicken Stock (see page 13)

4 tbsp golden raisins

salt

fresh cilantro sprigs, to garnish

NUTRITIONAL INFORMATION

Calories 329
Protein 14g
Carbohydrate 36g
Sugars 28g
Fat 15g
Saturates 2g

variation

Omit the raisins. Add 1 cored, sliced cooking apple with the vegetables and 1 tablespoon of dry unsweetened coconut with the spices in Step 2.

cook's tip

Curry paste is made from a mixture of spices, such as turmeric, fenugreek, and cumin. It comes in varying levels of spicy heat, so check you have chosen your preferred strength before you purchase.

1 Heat the oil in a large, heavy-bottomed pan. Add the chicken and cook over medium heat, turning frequently, for 10–15 minutes, or until golden brown all over. Transfer the chicken to a plate and reserve.

2 Add the vegetables to the pan and cook, stirring occasionally, for 10 minutes, or until just beginning to color. Stir in the curry paste, peppercorns, and cloves and cook, stirring constantly, for 1 minute.

3 Stir in the lentils, pour in the Stock, and bring to a boil. Return the chicken to the pan with the golden raisins, cover, and simmer over low heat for 1¼–1½ hours.

4 Remove the chicken from the pan. Remove and discard the skin and cut the flesh into bite-size pieces. Return them to the pan to heat through and season to taste with salt. Ladle the soup into warmed bowls, garnish with fresh cilantro sprigs, and serve.

umbrian onion soup

serves 4   **prep: 20 mins** ⏲   **cook: 1 hr** ♨

Like traditional Genoese Fish Soup (see page 30), this is a substantial and warming country soup which originally comes from northern Italy. Serve it with plenty of fresh, crusty bread.

INGREDIENTS

1 lb 9 oz/700 g onions

4 oz/115 g rindless lean bacon or pancetta, chopped

2 tbsp unsalted butter

2 tbsp olive oil

2 tsp sugar

salt and pepper

5 cups Chicken Stock (see page 13)

12 oz/350 g plum tomatoes, peeled and chopped

12 fresh basil leaves

freshly grated Parmesan cheese, to serve

NUTRITIONAL INFORMATION

Calories	.300
Protein	.7g
Carbohydrate	.19g
Sugars	.15g
Fat	.23g
Saturates	.9g

cook's tip

The best onions to use for this soup are sweet white Italian onions. These have a very mild flavor, which complements the other ingredients perfectly.

1 Thinly slice the onions and reserve. Place the bacon in a large, heavy-bottomed pan and cook over low heat, stirring, for 5 minutes, or until the fat begins to run. Add the butter, oil, onions, sugar, and a pinch of salt and stir to mix. Cover and cook, stirring occasionally, for 15–20 minutes, or until the onions are golden brown.

2 Pour in the Stock, add the tomatoes, and season to taste. Cover and simmer, stirring occasionally, for 30 minutes.

3 Tear 8 of the basil leaves into pieces and stir into the soup, then taste and adjust the seasoning, if necessary. Ladle the soup into warmed bowls, garnish with the remaining basil leaves, and serve, handing the Parmesan cheese round separately.

potato, carrot & leek soup

⏱ **cook: 45 mins**   ⏱ **prep: 10 mins**   **serves 4**

Once you have tried this thick, rich, substantial soup, it is sure to become a family favorite for its creamy taste and velvety texture. There is also an added bonus—it is easy and inexpensive to make.

NUTRITIONAL INFORMATION	
Calories 317	
Protein 5g	
Carbohydrate 31g	
Sugars 9g	
Fat 20g	
Saturates 13g	

INGREDIENTS

2 tbsp butter

3 potatoes, chopped

3 carrots, chopped

3 leeks, chopped

5 cups Chicken Stock
(see page 13)

½ tsp sugar

½ tsp freshly grated nutmeg

salt and pepper

3 tbsp heavy cream, plus extra
to garnish

cook's tip

This soup is also delicious made with leftover stock from boiling a side of bacon or gammon, or made with Beef Stock (see page 13).

1 Melt the butter in a large, heavy-bottomed pan. Add the potatoes, carrots, and leeks and cook over low heat, stirring occasionally, for 10 minutes.

2 Pour in the Stock and bring to a boil. Reduce the heat, partially cover the pan, and simmer for 30 minutes, or until the vegetables are tender. Remove the mixture from the heat and let cool slightly.

3 Pour the mixture into a blender or food processor and process until smooth. Return the soup to the rinsed-out pan, then stir in the sugar and nutmeg and season to taste with salt and pepper. Return to the heat and stir in the cream. Ladle the soup into warmed bowls and serve immediately, garnished with a swirl of cream.

corn, potato & cheese soup

⏱ **cook: 12–15 mins**   ⏳ **prep: 20 mins**   **serves 4**

NUTRITIONAL INFORMATION	
Calories	.860
Protein	16g
Carbohydrate	.54g
Sugars	.15g
Fat	.66g
Saturates	.41g

variation

If you can't find fresh sage, substitute a pinch of dried sage for the chopped leaves in Step 3 and omit the garnish.

This easy-to-make, satisfying soup is put together using ingredients from the pantry. It is the perfect choice for a Sunday brunch, as it takes very little effort or concentration.

INGREDIENTS

2 shallots, finely chopped

8 oz/225 g potatoes, diced

4 tbsp all-purpose flour

2 tbsp dry white wine

1¼ cups milk

11½ oz/325 g canned corn kernels, drained

generous ¾ cup grated Swiss cheese or Cheddar cheese

8–10 fresh sage leaves, chopped

generous 1¾ cups heavy cream

fresh sage sprigs, to garnish

CROUTONS

2–3 slices of day-old white bread

2 tbsp olive oil

cook's tip

When you are cooking croutons, make sure the oil is very hot before adding the bread cubes, otherwise the cubes may turn out soggy rather than crisp.

1 To make the croutons, cut the crusts off the bread slices, then cut the remaining bread into ¼-inch/5-mm squares. Heat the olive oil in a heavy-bottomed skillet and add the bread cubes. Cook, tossing and stirring constantly, until evenly colored. Drain the croutons thoroughly on paper towels and reserve.

2 Melt the butter in a large, heavy-bottomed pan. Add the shallots and cook over low heat, stirring occasionally, for 5 minutes, or until softened. Add the potatoes and cook, stirring, for 2 minutes.

3 Sprinkle in the flour and cook, stirring, for 1 minute. Remove the pan from the heat and stir in the white wine, then gradually stir in the milk. Return the pan to the heat and bring to a boil stirring constantly, then reduce the heat and simmer.

4 Stir in the corn kernels, cheese, chopped sage, and cream and heat through gently until the cheese has just melted. Ladle the soup into warmed bowls, scatter over the croutons, garnish with fresh sage sprigs, and serve.

roasted vegetable soup

serves 6   **prep: 15 mins, plus** 🕒 **10 mins cooling**   **cook: 1 hr 10 mins** 🕒

Mediterranean vegetables, roasted in olive oil and flavored with thyme, are the basis for this delicious, creamy soup.

INGREDIENTS

2–3 tbsp olive oil

1 lb 9 oz/700 g ripe tomatoes, peeled, cored, and halved

3 large yellow bell peppers, halved, cored, and seeded

3 zucchini, halved lengthwise

1 small eggplant, halved lengthwise

4 garlic cloves, halved

2 onions, cut into eighths

salt and pepper

pinch of dried thyme

4 cups Vegetable Stock (see page 13)

½ cup light cream

shredded fresh basil leaves, to garnish

NUTRITIONAL INFORMATION

Calories	130
Protein	3g
Carbohydrate	11g
Sugars	9g
Fat	9g
Saturates	3g

variation

The vegetables described give the best color combination, but red bell peppers work just as well. Green bell peppers are too bitter for this soup.

cook's tip

If you do not have a food processor, you can simply chop the roasted vegetables finely by hand in Step 3. Place them in a bowl and mix thoroughly before placing in the pan.

1 Preheat the oven to 375°F/190°C. Brush a large, shallow baking dish with olive oil. Arrange the tomatoes, bell peppers, zucchini, and eggplant across the bottom, cut-side down, in one layer. Tuck the garlic cloves and onion pieces into the gaps and drizzle the vegetables with oil. Season with salt and pepper and sprinkle with the thyme.

2 Bake the vegetables in the oven, uncovered, for 30–35 minutes, or until soft and browned around the edges. Let cool, then scrape out the eggplant flesh and reserve. Remove the skin from the bell peppers.

3 Working in batches, place the eggplant and bell pepper flesh in a food processor with the zucchini, tomatoes, garlic, and onion and chop to the consistency of salsa or pickle. Do not blend into a paste.

4 Place the chopped vegetable mixture in a pan, stir in the Stock, and simmer over medium heat for 20–30 minutes, until the vegetables are tender.

5 Stir in the cream and simmer the soup over low heat for 5 minutes, stirring occasionally, until hot. Taste and adjust the seasoning, if necessary. Ladle the soup into warmed soup bowls, garnish with basil, and serve.

broccoli & stilton soup

serves 4   **prep: 15 mins** ⏲   **cook: 30 mins** ☕

This soup looks pretty, smells wonderful, and tastes absolutely fabulous—just the thing for a midweek supper, or you could serve it with crackers and cheese for a filling weekend lunch.

INGREDIENTS

2 tbsp butter

1 leek, chopped

1 onion, chopped

12 oz/350 g broccoli, cut into florets

1 potato, chopped

2½ cups Chicken Stock

(see page 13)

1¼ cups milk

3 tbsp heavy cream

salt and pepper

5 oz/140 g Stilton cheese, crumbled

NUTRITIONAL INFORMATION	
Calories 407
Protein 16g
Carbohydrate 17g
Sugars 9g
Fat 31g
Saturates 19g

cook's tip

Be careful not to add too much salt when seasoning the soup in Step 3—the crumbled Stilton is likely to have made it quite salty already.

1 Melt the butter in a large pan. Add the leek and onion and cook over low heat, stirring, for 5 minutes, or until softened. Reserve 2–3 broccoli florets for the garnish and stir in the remainder with the potato.

2 Pour in the Stock, bring to a boil, then cover and simmer for 20 minutes, or until the vegetables are tender. Remove from the heat and let cool slightly. Pour the mixture into a blender or food processor and process to a smooth paste. Push the paste through a strainer with the back of a wooden spoon into the rinsed-out pan.

3 Add the milk and cream and season to taste with salt and pepper. Re-heat the soup gently. Meanwhile, blanch the reserved broccoli florets in boiling water for 30 seconds. Drain and refresh under cold running water, then slice thinly. When the soup is hot, stir in the cheese until it has just melted. Ladle the soup into warmed bowls, garnish with the broccoli florets, and serve immediately.

avgolemono

cook: 25–30 mins   **prep: 15 mins**   **serves 4**

The trick with this simple, classic Greek soup is not to let it boil once you have added the eggs. Otherwise they will curdle into an unpalatable mess in the pan and spoil the texture of the soup.

NUTRITIONAL INFORMATION	
Calories	.87
Protein	.4g
Carbohydrate	.12g
Sugars	.0g
Fat	.3g
Saturates	.1g

INGREDIENTS

5 cups Chicken Stock
(see page 13)
1 tbsp finely grated lemon rind
1 fresh thyme sprig
1 fresh parsley sprig
¼ cup long-grain rice
salt and pepper
2 eggs
2 tbsp lemon juice
fresh thyme sprigs, to garnish

cook's tip

This soup is sometimes served as a sauce with meatballs. To make avgolemono for this purpose, you should omit the rice in Step 2.

1 Pour the Stock into a large pan, add the lemon rind, thyme, and parsley and bring to a boil.

2 Add the rice, and season. Return to the boil, reduce the heat, and simmer for 15–20 minutes, or until the rice is tender. Remove the pan from the heat and let cool slightly.

3 Beat the eggs with the lemon juice. Whisk in a ladleful of the hot, but not boiling Stock. Whisk the egg and stock mixture into the pan and simmer over very low heat, whisking constantly, until thickened. Do not let the soup boil. Taste and adjust the seasoning, if necessary. Remove and discard the thyme and parsley sprigs, then ladle the soup into warmed bowls. Garnish with fresh thyme sprigs and serve immediately.

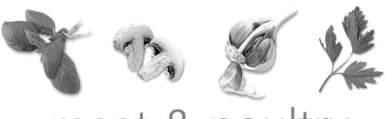

meat & poultry

This chapter is packed with main-meal recipes that are sure to tempt your appetite and set your taste buds tingling. There are rich, hearty stews, such as Daube of Beef (see page 54) and Louisiana Chicken (see page 104); traditional and classic dishes, such as Irish Stew (see page 67) and Chili con Carne (see page 56); quick and simple meals, such as Beef Stroganoff (see page 63) and Chicken Cacciatore (see page 103); and exotic combinations, such as Beef with Eggs (see page 62) and Lime & Coconut Lamb (see page 73). Whether your preference is for hot and spicy, rich and luxurious, or delicate and subtle flavors, you will be spoiled for choice.

Most of these dishes don't take long to prepare—one of the advantages of one-pot cooking. Some are also cooked quite quickly, while others can be left to their own devices, bubbling gently in the kitchen while you have a well-earned rest and a glass of wine before supper. Remember that most stews and casseroles taste even more flavorsome if they are allowed to cool after cooking and are re-heated the next day—and you still have only one pot to wash up.

This chapter features a wonderful collection of economical, filling, and tasty dishes that are ideal for midweek family suppers and Sunday lunches. Equally, you need look no further for some superb suggestions for entertaining in style—whether the sophisticated simplicity of Paprika Pork (see page 81), or the timeless elegance of Coq au Vin (see page 100).

beef in beer with herb dumplings

⏲ **cook: 2 hrs 30 mins**   ⏱ **prep: 25 mins**   **serves 6**

NUTRITIONAL INFORMATION

Calories	.576
Protein	.47g
Carbohydrate	.46g
Sugars	.18g
Fat	.22g
Saturates	.9g

variation

Substitute other root vegetables such as chopped parsnips or turnips for the sliced carrots, if you prefer.

Serve this traditional stew with its topping of satisfying dumplings to counteract even the coldest winter weather.

INGREDIENTS

STEW

2 tbsp corn oil

2 large onions, thinly sliced

8 carrots, sliced

4 tbsp all-purpose flour

salt and pepper

2 lb 12 oz/1.25 kg stewing steak, cut into cubes

generous 1¾ cups stout

2 tsp brown sugar

2 bay leaves

1 tbsp chopped fresh thyme

HERB DUMPLINGS

generous ¾ cup self-rising flour

pinch of salt

½ cup shredded suet

2 tbsp chopped fresh parsley, plus extra to garnish

about 4 tbsp water

cook's tip

Dumplings can be given a little added spice by mixing in a teaspoon of mustard powder with the flour—a delicious complement to any tasty stew.

1 Preheat the oven to 325°F/160°C. Heat the oil in a flameproof casserole. Add the onions and carrots and cook over low heat, stirring occasionally, for 5 minutes, or until the onions are softened. Meanwhile, place the flour in a plastic bag and season with salt and pepper. Add the stewing steak to the bag, tie the top, and shake well to coat. Do this in batches, if necessary.

2 Remove the vegetables from the casserole with a perforated spoon and reserve. Add the stewing steak to the casserole, in batches, and cook, stirring frequently, until browned all over. Return all the meat and the onions and carrots to the casserole and sprinkle in any remaining seasoned flour. Pour in the stout and add the sugar, bay leaves, and thyme. Bring to a boil, cover, and transfer to the preheated oven to bake for 1¾ hours.

3 To make the herb dumplings, sift the flour and salt into a bowl. Stir in the suet and parsley and add enough of the water to make a soft dough. Shape into small balls between the palms of your hands. Add to the casserole and return to the oven for 30 minutes. Remove and discard the bay leaves and serve, sprinkled with parsley.

daube of beef

serves 6 **prep: 20 mins,** plus 8 hrs marinating **cook: 3 hrs 15 mins**

A daube is a traditional French dish, in which meat was braised in a single piece, usually in wine. Once, it was cooked in a special pot placed over an open fire. Hot charcoal could be placed in the lid, so that the stew was cooked from both ends. Nowadays, an oven is easier and the meat is usually cut into cubes.

INGREDIENTS

1½ cups dry white wine	1 bay leaf
2 tbsp brandy	salt
1 tbsp white wine vinegar	1 lb 10 oz/750 g beef topside, cut
4 shallots, sliced	into 1-inch/2.5-cm cubes
4 carrots, sliced	2 tbsp olive oil
1 garlic clove, finely chopped	1 lb 12 oz/800 g canned
6 black peppercorns	chopped tomatoes
4 fresh thyme sprigs	8 oz/225 g mushrooms, sliced
1 fresh rosemary sprig	strip of finely pared orange rind
2 fresh parsley sprigs, plus	2 oz/55 g Bayonne ham, cut into strips
extra to garnish	12 black olives

NUTRITIONAL INFORMATION

Calories	319
Protein	31g
Carbohydrate	10g
Sugars	9g
Fat	12g
Saturates	4g

variation

Bayonne ham is a dry-cured, smoked ham from the Basses-Pyrénées. If it is not available, substitute prosciutto.

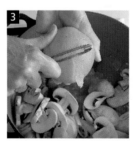

cook's tip

When you add citrus rind to a casserole, it is a good idea to grate or pare it directly into the casserole. If you prepare it too far in advance, it may dry out and lose some of its flavor.

1 Combine the wine, brandy, vinegar, shallots, carrots, garlic, peppercorns, thyme, rosemary, parsley, and bay leaf and season to taste with salt. Add the beef, stirring to coat, then cover with plastic wrap and let marinate in the refrigerator for 8 hours, or overnight.

2 Preheat the oven to 300°F/150°C. Drain the beef, reserving the marinade, and pat dry on paper towels. Heat half the oil in a large, flameproof casserole. Add the beef cubes in batches and cook over medium heat, stirring, for 3–4 minutes, or until browned. Transfer the beef to a plate with a perforated spoon. Brown the remaining beef, adding more oil, if necessary.

3 Return all of the beef to the casserole and add the tomatoes and their juices, mushrooms, and orange rind. Strain the reserved marinade into the casserole. Bring to a boil, cover, and cook in the oven for 2½ hours.

4 Remove the casserole from the oven, add the ham and olives, and return it to the oven to cook for an additional 30 minutes, or until the beef is very tender. Discard the orange rind and serve straight from the casserole, garnished with parsley.

chili con carne

serves 4   **prep: 15 mins** ⏲   **cook: 30–35 mins** ⏲

This Tex-Mex favorite is often served with rice, but it is just as delicious with tortillas or thick slices of crusty bread. Buy ready-made tortillas and heat them through in a dry skillet.

INGREDIENTS

2 tbsp corn oil

1 lb 2 oz/500 g fresh ground beef

1 large onion, chopped

1 garlic clove, finely chopped

1 green bell pepper, seeded and diced

1 tsp chili powder

1 lb 12 oz/800 g canned
chopped tomatoes

1 lb 12 oz/800 g canned red kidney
beans, drained and rinsed

scant 2 cups Beef Stock (see page 13)

salt

handful of fresh cilantro sprigs

2 tbsp sour cream, to serve

NUTRITIONAL INFORMATION	
Calories 437	
Protein 41g	
Carbohydrate 43g	
Sugars 16g	
Fat 13g	
Saturates 3g	

variation

Substitute 1–2 finely chopped, seeded fresh chiles for the chili powder in Step 2. Anaheim (mild) or jalapeño (hot) are classic Tex-Mex varieties.

1 Heat the oil in a large, heavy-bottomed pan or flameproof casserole. Add the beef. Cook over medium heat, stirring frequently, for 5 minutes, or until broken up and browned.

2 Reduce the heat, add the onion, garlic, and bell pepper and cook, stirring frequently, for 10 minutes.

3 Stir in the chili powder, tomatoes and their juices, and kidney beans. Pour in the Stock and season with salt. Bring to a boil, reduce the heat and simmer, stirring frequently, for 15–20 minutes, or until the meat is tender.

4 Chop the cilantro sprigs, reserving a few for a garnish, and stir into the chili. Adjust the seasoning, if necessary. Either serve immediately with a splash of sour cream, and cilantro sprigs to garnish, or let cool, then store in the refrigerator overnight. Re-heating the chili the next day makes it more flavorsome.

simple savory beef

cook: 1 hr **prep: 10 mins** **serves 4**

It is always worth buying the best-quality ground beef you can afford, as it will be leaner. This is not only healthier, but is also tastier and more economical, as less fat will be released during cooking.

NUTRITIONAL INFORMATION

Calories	.286
Protein	.26g
Carbohydrate	.21g
Sugars	.9g
Fat	.12g
Saturates	.3g

INGREDIENTS

2 tbsp peanut or corn oil

1 lb/450 g fresh ground beef

1 small onion, chopped

½ green bell pepper, seeded and chopped

11½ oz/325 g canned corn
kernels, drained

7 oz/200 g canned tomatoes

2 tsp chopped fresh thyme

1¼ cups Beef Stock (see page 13)
or 1 beef stock cube dissolved in
1¼ cups boiling water

salt and pepper

fresh thyme sprigs, to garnish

cook's tip

You could serve this dish with plain boiled rice, but if you don't want to bother with a second pot, serve with crusty rolls and salad greens.

1 Heat the oil in a heavy-bottomed pan. Add the beef. Cook over medium heat, stirring, for 5 minutes, or until broken up and browned. Drain off any excess fat.

2 Add the onion, bell pepper, corn, tomatoes and their juices, and chopped thyme. Pour in the Stock and bring the mixture to a boil, stirring constantly.

3 Reduce the heat, cover, and simmer for 50 minutes. Season to taste with salt and pepper, garnish with fresh thyme sprigs, and serve immediately.

stifado

cook: 2 hrs 15 mins   **prep: 15 mins**   **serves 6**

NUTRITIONAL INFORMATION

Calories 270

Protein 29g

Carbohydrate 21g

Sugars 7g

Fat 8g

Saturates 2g

variation

If you want to prepare this stew quickly, without making a stock, substitute water for the Beef Stock.

This wonderful traditional Greek stew is cooked very slowly with the result that the beef almost melts in the mouth and all the flavors mingle in a rich, thick, delicious gravy.

INGREDIENTS

1 lb/450 g tomatoes, peeled

⅔ cup Beef Stock (see page 13)

2 tbsp olive oil

1 lb/450 g shallots, peeled

2 garlic cloves, finely chopped

1 lb 9 oz/700 g stewing steak, cut into 1-inch/2.5-cm cubes

1 fresh rosemary sprig

1 bay leaf

2 tbsp red wine vinegar

salt and pepper

1 lb/450 g potatoes, cut into fourths

cook's tip

Fresh, uncooked rosemary sprigs and bay leaves would make an attractive garnish for this dish, but remember to remove them before eating.

1 Place the tomatoes in a blender or food processor, add the Stock, and process to a paste. Alternatively, push them through a strainer into a bowl with the back of a wooden spoon and mix with the Stock.

2 Heat the oil in a large, heavy-bottomed pan or flameproof casserole. Add the shallots and garlic and cook over low heat, stirring occasionally, for 8 minutes, or until golden. Transfer to a plate with a perforated spoon. Add the steak to the pan and cook, stirring frequently, for 5–8 minutes, or until browned.

3 Return the shallots and garlic to the pan, add the tomato mixture, herbs, and vinegar and season to taste with salt and pepper. Cover and simmer gently for 1½ hours. Add the potatoes, re-cover, and simmer for an additional 30 minutes. Remove and discard the rosemary and bay leaf and serve immediately.

beef goulash

serves 4 **prep: 10 mins** **cook: 2 hrs 15 mins**

Slow, gentle cooking is the secret to this superb goulash—which makes a warming, comforting meal on a cold evening. Rice is the ideal accompaniment to absorb the rich flavors.

INGREDIENTS

2 tbsp vegetable oil

1 large onion, chopped

1 garlic clove, crushed

1 lb 10 oz/750 g lean stewing steak

2 tbsp paprika

15 oz/425 g canned chopped tomatoes

2 tbsp tomato paste

1 large red bell pepper, seeded and chopped

6 oz/175 g mushrooms, sliced

2½ cups Beef Stock (see page 13)

1 tbsp cornstarch

1 tbsp water

salt and pepper

chopped fresh parsley, to garnish

long-grain rice and wild rice, to serve

NUTRITIONAL INFORMATION	
Calories	.386
Protein	.44g
Carbohydrate	.17g
Sugars	.10g
Fat	.16g
Saturates	.5g

variation

To make a side dressing of yogurt, place 4 tablespoons of plain yogurt in a serving bowl, sprinkle with a little paprika, and serve with the goulash.

cook's tip

Wild rice can be expensive, so combining it with a cheaper rice not only gives a little color variation to this dish, but also makes it economical.

1 Heat the vegetable oil in a large, heavy-bottomed skillet. Add the onion and garlic and cook over low heat for 3–4 minutes.

2 Using a sharp knife, cut the steak into chunks, add to the skillet, and cook over high heat for 3 minutes, or until browned. Add the paprika and stir well, then add the tomatoes, tomato paste, bell pepper, and mushrooms. Cook for an additional 2 minutes, stirring frequently. Pour in the Stock. Bring to a boil, reduce the heat, cover, and simmer for 1½–2 hours, or until the meat is tender.

3 Blend the cornstarch and water together in a small bowl, then add to the skillet, stirring, until thickened and smooth. Cook for 1 minute. Season to taste with salt and pepper.

4 Transfer the beef goulash to a warmed serving dish, garnish with chopped fresh parsley, and serve with a mix of long-grain and wild rice.

beef with eggs

serves 4 **prep: 10 mins** ⟲ **cook: 10–15 mins** ⟳

This delicacy comes from Thailand, although similar recipes exist in the cuisines of other Asian countries. Only one pan is used, although the dish is cooked in individual ramekins.

INGREDIENTS

4 oz/115 g sirloin steak, finely chopped

1 tsp grated fresh gingerroot

1 tbsp Thai fish sauce

pepper

3 eggs

½ cup Chicken Stock (see page 13)

3 scallions, finely chopped

4 whole scallions, to garnish

NUTRITIONAL INFORMATION

Calories 124
Protein 12g
Carbohydrate 1g
Sugars 0g
Fat 8g
Saturates 2g

cook's tip

If you are going to serve this dish as an appetizer, this quantity is enough for 6 people. If you don't have time to make a stock, use water instead.

1 Combine the steak, gingerroot, and Thai fish sauce in a bowl and season to taste with pepper.

2 Beat the eggs with the Stock in a separate bowl. Stir the egg mixture into the steak mixture and add the scallions. Whisk well to blend.

3 Set a steamer over a pan of gently simmering water. Pour the steak and egg mixture into 4 ramekins and place them in the steamer. Cover and steam for 10–15 minutes, or until set. Remove from the steamer and let cool slightly before serving. Garnish with the whole scallions.

beef stroganoff

cook: 25 mins

prep: 15 mins, plus 20 mins soaking

serves 4

This traditional Slavic recipe makes a comforting meal on a chilly evening. Thin, delicately cooked beef and a mustard and cream sauce make this straightforward dish taste out-of-the-ordinary.

NUTRITIONAL INFORMATION	
Calories	.354
Protein	.20g
Carbohydrate	.6g
Sugars	.3g
Fat	.28g
Saturates	.14g

INGREDIENTS

½ oz/15 g dried ceps

12 oz/350 g beef fillet

2 tbsp olive oil

4 oz/115 g shallots, sliced

6 oz/175 g cremini mushrooms

salt and pepper

½ tsp Dijon mustard

5 tbsp heavy cream

fresh chives, to garnish

freshly cooked pasta, to serve

cook's tip

Ceps, also known as porcini, are widely available from large supermarkets and delicatessens. You could use other dried wild mushrooms instead, if you prefer.

1 Place the dried ceps in a bowl and cover with hot water. Let soak for 20 minutes. Meanwhile, cut the beef against the grain into ¼-inch/5-mm thick slices, then into ½-inch/1-cm long strips, and reserve.

2 Drain the mushrooms, reserving the soaking liquid, and chop. Strain the soaking liquid through a fine-mesh strainer or coffee filter and reserve.

3 Heat half the oil in a large skillet. Add the shallots and cook over low heat, stirring occasionally, for 5 minutes, or until softened. Add the dried mushrooms, reserved soaking water, and whole cremini mushrooms and cook, stirring frequently, for 10 minutes, or until almost all of the liquid has evaporated, then transfer the mixture to a plate.

4 Heat the remaining oil in the skillet, add the beef and cook, stirring frequently, for 4 minutes, or until browned all over. You may need to do this in batches. Return the mushroom mixture to the skillet and season to taste with salt and pepper. Place the mustard and cream in a small bowl and stir to mix, then fold into the mixture. Heat through gently, then serve with freshly cooked pasta, garnished with chives.

sweet & sour venison stir-fry

cook: 15 mins **prep: 15 mins** **serves 4**

NUTRITIONAL INFORMATION	
Calories	219
Protein	23g
Carbohydrate	20g
Sugars	18g
Fat	5g
Saturates	1g

Venison is super-lean and low in fat, so it's the perfect choice for a healthy diet. Cooked quickly with crisp vegetables, it makes an ideal ingredient for a light, tasty stir-fry.

INGREDIENTS

12 oz/350 g lean venison steak

1 bunch of scallions

1 red bell pepper

3½ oz/100 g snow peas

3½ oz/100 g baby corn cobs

1 tbsp vegetable oil

1 garlic clove, crushed

1-inch/2.5-cm piece fresh gingerroot, finely chopped

3 tbsp light soy sauce, plus extra for dipping

1 tbsp white wine vinegar

2 tbsp dry sherry

2 tsp clear honey

8 oz/225 g canned pineapple pieces in natural juice, drained

¼ cup bean sprouts

freshly cooked rice, to serve

variation

For a meal-in-one, cook 8 oz/225 g of egg noodles and add to the wok in Step 4 with the bean sprouts and an extra 2 tablespoons of soy sauce.

cook's tip

Wild venison has a very strong flavor, and can become tough when cooked. Buy farmed venison for this recipe, which is more tender and has a lighter flavor.

1 Trim any fat from the venison and cut into thin strips. Cut the scallions into 1-inch/2.5-cm pieces. Halve and seed the red bell pepper and cut into 1-inch/2.5-cm pieces. Trim the snow peas and baby corn.

2 Heat the vegetable oil in a preheated wok or large skillet over high heat. Add the venison, garlic, and gingerroot and stir-fry for 5 minutes. Add the scallions, red bell pepper, snow peas, and baby corn cobs, then stir in the soy sauce, vinegar, sherry, and honey. Stir-fry for an additional 5 minutes.

3 Carefully stir in the pineapple pieces and bean sprouts and cook for an additional 1–2 minutes to heat through. Serve with freshly cooked rice and extra soy sauce for dipping.

lamb with pears

serves 4 **prep: 10 mins** ⏲ **cook: 2 hrs** ⏲

A rich and often quite fatty meat, lamb is usually partnered with sharp fruit, such as redcurrants, or tangy mint to bring out its flavor. This unusual combination is just as delicious.

INGREDIENTS

1 tbsp olive oil

2 lb 4 oz/1 kg best end-of-neck lamb cutlets, trimmed of visible fat

6 pears, peeled, cored, and cut into fourths

1 tsp ground ginger

4 potatoes, diced

4 tbsp hard cider

salt and pepper

1 lb/450 g green beans

2 tbsp snipped fresh chives, to garnish

NUTRITIONAL INFORMATION

Calories	.504
Protein	.37g
Carbohydrate	.53g
Sugars	.27g
Fat	.17g
Saturates	.7g

cook's tip

Look for pears that are still firm even when ripe, such as Beurre Dumont, Forelle, or Williams. Soft pears will begin to disintegrate during the cooking process.

1 Preheat the oven to 325°F/160°C. Heat the olive oil in a flameproof casserole over medium heat. Add the lamb and cook, turning frequently, for 5–10 minutes, or until browned on all sides.

2 Arrange the pear pieces on top, then sprinkle over the ginger. Cover with the potatoes. Pour in the cider and season to taste with salt and pepper. Cover and cook in the preheated oven for 1¼ hours.

3 Trim the stem ends of the green beans. Remove the casserole from the oven and add the beans, then re-cover and return to the oven for an additional 30 minutes. Taste and adjust the seasoning and sprinkle with the chives. Serve immediately.

irish stew

⏲ **cook: 2 hrs 30 mins**   ⏱ **prep: 10 mins**   **serves 4**

Nothing could be simpler, tastier, or more economical than this traditional, heart-warming stew. Serve with fresh soda bread for an authentic touch—and to mop up the delicious juices.

NUTRITIONAL INFORMATION	
Calories	.496
Protein	.40g
Carbohydrate	.55g
Sugars	.16g
Fat	.15g
Saturates	.6g

INGREDIENTS

4 tbsp all-purpose flour

salt and pepper

3 lb/1.3 kg middle neck of lamb, trimmed of visible fat

3 large onions, chopped

3 carrots, sliced

1 lb/450 g potatoes, cut into fourths

½ tsp dried thyme

scant 3½ cups hot Beef Stock (see page 13)

2 tbsp chopped fresh parsley, to garnish

cook's tip

This stew is even more substantial and flavorsome if it is served with Herb Dumplings (see page 53). Add them to the casserole 30 minutes before the end of the cooking time.

1 Preheat the oven to 325°F/160°C. Spread the flour on a plate and season with salt and pepper. Roll the pieces of lamb in the flour to coat, shaking off any excess, and arrange in the bottom of a casserole.

2 Layer the onions, carrots, and potatoes on top of the lamb.

3 Sprinkle in the thyme and pour in the Stock, then cover and cook in the preheated oven for 2½ hours. Garnish with the chopped parsley and serve straight from the casserole.

french country casserole

serves 6   **prep: 15 mins** ⌚   **cook: 2 hrs 15 mins** ♨

A crispy potato topping covers a dish of succulent, tender lamb, flavored with mint, leeks, and apricots in this traditional rustic casserole—which looks as good as it tastes.

INGREDIENTS

2 tbsp corn oil	1 tbsp tomato paste
4 lb 8 oz/2 kg boneless leg of lamb, cut	1 tbsp sugar
into 1-inch/2.5-cm cubes	2 tbsp chopped fresh mint
6 leeks, sliced	4 oz/115 g dried apricots, chopped
1 tbsp all-purpose flour	salt and pepper
⅔ cup rosé wine	2 lb 4 oz/1 kg potatoes, sliced
1¼ cups Chicken Stock	3 tbsp melted unsalted butter
(see page 13)	fresh mint sprigs, to garnish

NUTRITIONAL INFORMATION

Calories	.720
Protein	.60g
Carbohydrate	.44g
Sugars	.15g
Fat	.33g
Saturates	.15g

variation

Use a light red wine instead of rosé if you would prefer a slightly heavier flavor in this country casserole.

cook's tip

It is always a good idea to cook meat briefly to brown it before adding it to a casserole. This will ensure that it has an appetizing color in the finished dish.

1 Preheat the oven to 350°F/180°C. Heat the oil in a large, flameproof casserole. Add the lamb in batches and cook over medium heat, stirring, for 5–8 minutes, or until browned. Transfer to a plate.

2 Add the sliced leeks to the casserole and cook, stirring occasionally, for 5 minutes, or until softened. Sprinkle in the flour and cook, stirring, for 1 minute. Pour in the wine and Stock and bring to a boil, stirring. Stir in the tomato paste, sugar, chopped mint, and apricots and season to taste with salt and pepper.

3 Return the lamb to the casserole and stir. Arrange the potato slices on top and brush with the melted butter. Cover and bake in the preheated oven for 1½ hours.

4 Increase the oven temperature to 400°F/ 200°C, uncover the casserole, and bake for an additional 30 minutes, or until the potato topping is golden brown. Serve immediately, garnished with fresh mint sprigs.

lamb & potato moussaka

🕐 **cook: 1 hr 15 mins**

🕐 **prep: 20 mins, plus 20 mins standing**

serves 4 ✕ 3

NUTRITIONAL INFORMATION

Calories 422

Protein 32g

Carbohydrate 35g

Sugars 8g

Fat 18g

Saturates 8g

variation

To ring the changes in this moussaka recipe, substitute ground beef for the lamb, and use beef-flavored stock.

Ground lamb makes a very tasty and authentic moussaka— a traditional Greek meat and vegetable pie.

INGREDIENTS

1 large eggplant, sliced

salt and pepper

1 tbsp olive oil

1 onion, finely chopped

1 garlic clove, crushed

12 oz/350 g fresh lean ground lamb

9 oz/250 g mushrooms, sliced

15 oz/425 g canned chopped tomatoes with herbs

⅔ cup lamb stock

2 tbsp cornstarch

2 tbsp water

1 lb 2 oz/500 g potatoes, parboiled for 10 minutes and sliced

2 eggs

generous ½ cup lowfat soft cheese

⅔ cup lowfat plain yogurt

½ cup grated lowfat mature Cheddar cheese

fresh flatleaf parsley sprigs, to garnish

salad greens, to serve

cook's tip

You do not have to use a meat stock for this moussaka— a good quality Vegetable Stock (see page 13) works just as well.

1 Preheat the oven to 375°F/190°C. Lay the eggplant slices on a clean board and sprinkle with salt. Let stand for 10 minutes, then turn the slices over and repeat. Place in a colander, rinse, and drain.

2 While the eggplants are standing, heat the oil in a large pan. Add the onion and garlic and cook for 3–4 minutes. Add the lamb and mushrooms and cook over medium heat for 5 minutes, or until browned. Stir in the tomatoes and stock, bring to a boil, and simmer for 10 minutes. Mix the cornstarch and water together to make a smooth paste, then stir into the pan. Cook, stirring constantly, until thickened.

3 Spoon half the mixture into an ovenproof dish. Cover with the eggplant slices, then the remaining lamb mixture. Arrange the sliced potatoes on top.

4 Beat the eggs, soft cheese, and yogurt together. Season to taste with salt and pepper, then pour over the potatoes to cover.

Sprinkle over the cheese and bake in the preheated oven for 45 minutes, or until the topping is set and golden brown. Garnish with flatleaf parsley sprigs and serve with salad greens.

moroccan lamb

serves 4 **prep: 20 mins** ⏲ **cook: 1 hr 30 mins** ⏲

Slow-cooking lamb with dried fruit and spices is traditional in North Africa and stews flavored with dried apricots have become familiar elsewhere, but other dried fruit are also used, like prunes.

INGREDIENTS

1 lb 2 oz/500 g boneless leg of lamb
dredge in flour
1 tbsp <u>corn oil</u>
12 oz/350 g shallots, peeled but left whole
generous 1¼ cups Chicken Stock (see page 13)
1 tbsp clear honey
1 tsp ground cinnamon
½ tsp ground ginger
½ tsp saffron threads, lightly crushed
¼ tsp freshly grated nutmeg
salt and pepper
grated rind and juice of 1 small orange, plus extra to garnish
12 no-soak dried prunes

NUTRITIONAL INFORMATION	
Calories 335
Protein 28g
Carbohydrate 26g
Sugars 24g
Fat 14g
Saturates 6g

cook's tip

"No-soak," dried fruit is the same thing as dried, but moist, "ready-to-eat" fruit, is also now available in small bags in most major food stores.

1 Cut the lamb into large cubes. Heat the oil in a flameproof casserole, add the lamb, and cook over medium heat, stirring, for 3–5 minutes, or until browned. Transfer to a plate. Add the shallots to the casserole and cook over low heat, stirring occasionally, for 10 minutes, or until golden. Transfer them to a separate plate with a perforated spoon.

2 Pour away any excess fat from the casserole, then add the Stock and bring to a boil, stirring constantly, and scraping up any sediment from the bottom. Return the lamb to the casserole and stir in the honey, cinnamon, ginger, saffron, and nutmeg. Season to taste with salt and pepper, cover, and simmer for 30 minutes.

3 Return the shallots to the casserole and add the orange rind and juice. Re-cover and simmer for an additional 30 minutes. Add the prunes and adjust the seasoning, if necessary. Simmer, uncovered, for an additional 15 minutes. Garnish with orange rind and serve immediately.

dredge in flour 1st
makes Kitchen v. smelly

bake in oven?
apricots

big pieces worked well

lime & coconut lamb

cook: 10 mins   **prep: 10 mins**   **serves 4**

This Thai-style curry is so delicious and tastes so authentic that your family will think you have spent hours preparing it. Only you will know just how speedy and simple it is.

NUTRITIONAL INFORMATION

Calories	273
Protein	25g
Carbohydrate	2g
Sugars	1g
Fat	19g
Saturates	5g

INGREDIENTS

1 lb/450 g lamb fillet

2 oz/55 g unsweetened coconut cream

1¼ cups boiling water

2 tsp peanut or corn oil

1–2 garlic cloves, finely chopped

2 tsp grated fresh gingerroot

2 tbsp Thai green curry paste

grated rind and juice of 1 lime

salt and pepper

2 tbsp chopped fresh cilantro, plus extra to garnish

freshly cooked rice, to serve

cook's tip

Good-quality, ready-made Thai curry pastes are available in major food stores and specialist Asian food stores, and add an authentic flavor to home-cooked Thai dishes.

1 Cut the lamb across the grain into strips about 1½ inches/4 cm long. Combine the coconut cream and boiling water in a bowl, stirring well to mix.

2 Heat the oil in a preheated wok or large skillet. Add the lamb, garlic, and gingerroot and cook over high heat for 2–3 minutes. Stir in the curry paste and coconut mixture and add the lime rind and juice. Season to taste with salt and pepper.

3 Bring the mixture to a boil, stirring constantly, then reduce the heat and simmer for 5 minutes. Stir in the chopped cilantro and serve with rice, sprinkled with extra chopped cilantro.

rogan josh

serves 6

prep: 20 mins,
plus 8 hrs marinating

cook: 1 hr 30 mins–
1 hr 45 mins

This richly colored, spicy dish is among the most popular lamb curries from India. It makes a filling family supper when served with a generous helping of spicy naan bread.

INGREDIENTS

scant 1 cup plain yogurt

3 tbsp lemon juice

1-inch/2.5-cm piece fresh
gingerroot, grated

2 garlic cloves, finely chopped

salt

2 lb/900 g lamb fillet, cut
into 1-inch/2.5-cm cubes

3 tbsp corn oil

½ tsp cumin seeds

4 cardamom pods

1 onion, finely chopped

1 fresh green chile, seeded and
finely chopped

2 tsp ground cumin

2 tsp ground coriander

14 oz/400 g canned chopped tomatoes

2 tbsp tomato paste

⅔ cup water

2 bay leaves, plus extra to garnish

NUTRITIONAL INFORMATION

Calories 340

Protein 35g

Carbohydrate 8g

Sugars 7g

Fat 19g

Saturates 7g

variation

Use a red chile instead of the green chile if you want the dish to have a slightly sweeter flavor.

cook's tip

When you cook chopped fresh chile in a hot skillet, stir frequently, and keep a close eye on it. Small pieces of chile burn easily, and will quickly turn black if left unattended.

1 Place the yogurt, lemon juice, gingerroot, and half the garlic in a nonmetallic dish and mix. Season well with salt. Add the lamb. Mix well, cover with plastic wrap, and let marinate in the refrigerator for 8 hours, or overnight.

2 Heat the oil in a large, heavy-bottomed skillet over high heat. Add the cumin seeds and cook, stirring, for 1–2 minutes, or until they begin to pop and release their aroma. Add the cardamom pods and cook, stirring constantly, for an additional 2 minutes. Add the onion, chile, and remaining garlic and cook, stirring frequently, for 5 minutes, or until the onion is softened. Stir in the ground cumin and coriander.

3 Add the lamb with the marinade and cook, stirring occasionally, for 5 minutes. Add the tomatoes and their juices, and the tomato paste, water, and bay leaves. Bring to a boil, stirring, then reduce the heat, cover, and simmer for 1¼–1½ hours, or until cooked through and tender. Garnish with bay leaves and serve.

lamb with mint

cook: 30 mins **prep: 10 mins** **serves 4**

NUTRITIONAL INFORMATION

Calories	.245
Protein	.21g
Carbohydrate	.10g
Sugars	.7g
Fat	.14g
Saturates	.4g

variation

If you prefer, use peeled, chopped, fresh tomatoes rather than canned tomatoes, but add 1 tablespoon of tomato paste with them in Step 3.

A classic combination popular in many different countries, this recipe is for a mildly spiced Indian dish of ground lamb, mixed with peas. Serve with naan bread or chapatis.

INGREDIENTS

2 tbsp corn oil	7 oz/200 g canned chopped tomatoes
1 onion, chopped	1 tbsp chopped fresh mint
1 garlic clove, finely chopped	3 oz/85 g fresh or frozen peas
1 tsp grated fresh gingerroot	2 carrots, sliced into thin sticks
1 tsp ground cilantro *coriander*	1 fresh green chile, seeded and
½ tsp chili powder	finely chopped
¼ tsp ground turmeric	1 tbsp chopped fresh cilantro
pinch of salt	fresh mint sprigs, to garnish
12 oz/350 g fresh ground lamb	

cook's tip

To ensure that the lamb is lean, buy boneless leg, trim off all of the visible fat, and grind it yourself, using a meat grinder or food processor.

1 Heat the oil in a large, heavy-bottomed skillet or flameproof casserole. Add the onion and cook over low heat, stirring occasionally, for 10 minutes, or until golden.

2 Meanwhile, place the garlic, gingerroot, ground cilantro, chili powder, turmeric, and salt in a small bowl and mix well. Add the spice mixture to the skillet and cook, stirring constantly, for 2 minutes. Add the lamb and cook, stirring frequently, for 8–10 minutes, or until it is broken up and browned.

3 Add the tomatoes and their juices, the mint, peas, carrots, chile, and fresh cilantro. Cook, stirring constantly, for 3–5 minutes, then serve, garnished with fresh mint sprigs.

five-spice lamb

serves 4   prep: 15 mins   cook: 12–15 mins

Chinese five-spice powder, gingerroot, and soy and hoisin sauces flavor this quick and easy aromatic stir-fry—an unusual, Eastern-style dish, which is a great idea for impressing guests.

INGREDIENTS

1 lb 7 oz/650 g lamb fillet

2 tbsp peanut or corn oil

1 onion, finely chopped

1 garlic clove, finely chopped

1 red bell pepper, seeded and
thinly sliced

1 yellow bell pepper, seeded and
thinly sliced

2 tsp grated fresh gingerroot

6 oz/175 g green beans, halved

1 tsp Chinese five-spice powder

1 tbsp hoisin sauce

1 tbsp dark soy sauce

4 tbsp Chinese rice wine
or dry sherry

GARNISH

2 tbsp chopped fresh cilantro

1 tbsp toasted sesame seeds

NUTRITIONAL INFORMATION

Calories 367

Protein 36g

Carbohydrate 7g

Sugars 5g

Fat 22g

Saturates 8g

variation

To add some spiciness, add 1–2 fresh red chiles, seeded and chopped, with the bell peppers and gingerroot in Step 2. Serve this dish with freshly cooked rice or egg noodles.

cook's tip

Chinese five-spice powder and rice wine are available from most major food stores and Chinese food stores. Note that the Chinese spice is different from Indian five-spice powder.

1 Cut the lamb across the grain into strips about 1½ inches/4 cm long. Heat the oil in a preheated wok or large skillet. Add the lamb and stir-fry over high heat for 4 minutes, or until browned all over. Transfer to a plate with a perforated spoon.

2 Add the onion, garlic, bell peppers, and fresh gingerroot to the wok and stir-fry for 3–4 minutes. Add the green beans and stir-fry for an additional 2 minutes.

3 Return the lamb to the wok, then stir in the Chinese five-spice powder, hoisin sauce, soy sauce, and Chinese rice wine. Cook, stirring and tossing the mixture constantly, until the lamb is tender and coated in the sauce. Serve, garnished with chopped cilantro and toasted sesame seeds.

pork chops with bell peppers & corn

serves 4 **prep: 10 mins**   **cook: 45 mins**

If you cook this luscious and simple dish on the hob, serve it with plenty of crusty bread. If you cook it in the oven (see Cook's Tip), serve it with baked potatoes. Either way, it makes a delicious meal.

INGREDIENTS

1 tbsp corn oil

4 pork chops, trimmed of visible fat

1 onion, chopped

1 garlic clove, finely chopped

1 green bell pepper, seeded and sliced

1 red bell pepper, seeded and sliced

11½ oz/325 g canned corn kernels

1 tbsp chopped fresh parsley

salt and pepper

mashed potato, to serve

NUTRITIONAL INFORMATION

Calories	.286
Protein	.24g
Carbohydrate	.25g
Sugars	.11g
Fat	.11g
Saturates	.3g

1 Heat the oil in a large, flameproof casserole. Add the pork chops in batches and cook over medium heat, turning occasionally, for 5 minutes, or until browned. Transfer the chops to a plate with a perforated spoon.

2 Add the chopped onion to the casserole and cook, stirring occasionally, for 5 minutes, or until softened. Add the garlic and bell peppers and cook, stirring occasionally, for an additional 5 minutes. Stir in the corn kernels and their juices and the parsley and season to taste.

3 Return the chops to the casserole, spooning the vegetable mixture over them. Cover and simmer for 30 minutes, or until tender. Serve immediately with mashed potato.

cook's tip

This casserole can also be cooked in a preheated oven, 350°F/180°C, for 30 minutes, or until tender. Bake some potatoes alongside as an accompaniment.

paprika pork

cook: 35 mins **prep: 20 mins** **serves 4**

This is a good dish for entertaining, as it can be prepared in advance and stored in the refrigerator for up to two days. To serve, reheat gently, then stir in the sour cream.

NUTRITIONAL INFORMATION

Calories	.478
Protein	.38g
Carbohydrate	.10g
Sugars	.4g
Fat	.30g
Saturates	.13g

INGREDIENTS

1 lb 8 oz/675 g pork fillet

2 tbsp corn oil

2 tbsp butter

1 onion, chopped

1 tbsp paprika

2½ tbsp all-purpose flour

1¼ cups Chicken Stock (see page 13)
or 1 chicken stock cube dissolved in
1¼ cups boiling water

4 tbsp dry sherry

4 oz/115 g mushrooms, sliced

salt and pepper

⅔ cup sour cream

cook's tip

There are 2 kinds of paprika—sweet and hot—but both are much milder than cayenne pepper. Sweet paprika is the best choice for this recipe.

1 Cut the pork into 1½-inch/4-cm cubes. Heat the oil and butter in a large pan. Add the pork and cook over medium heat, stirring, for 5 minutes, or until browned. Transfer to a plate with a perforated spoon.

2 Add the chopped onion to the pan and cook, stirring occasionally, for 5 minutes, or until softened. Stir in the paprika and flour and cook, stirring constantly, for 2 minutes. Gradually stir in the Stock and bring to a boil, stirring constantly.

3 Return the pork to the pan, add the sherry and sliced mushrooms, and season to taste with salt and pepper. Cover and simmer gently for 20 minutes, or until the pork is tender. Stir in the sour cream and serve.

pot-roast pork

⏲ **cook: 1 hr 30 mins**   ⏲ **prep: 20 mins**   **serves 4**

NUTRITIONAL INFORMATION	
Calories	.850
Protein	.41g
Carbohydrate	.12g
Sugars	.4g
Fat	.70g
Saturates	.33g

variation

Substitute 2 thinly sliced fennel bulbs for the chopped celery if you would prefer an aniseed flavor in this dish.

Beef and chicken are the most popular choices for pot-roasting, but a loin of pork works superbly well, too. This is a rich and flavorsome dish that is ideal for entertaining.

INGREDIENTS

1 tbsp corn oil	⅔ cup dry cider
¼ cup butter	⅔ cup Chicken Stock
2 lb 4 oz/1 kg boned and	(see page 13) or water
rolled pork loin	salt and pepper
4 shallots, chopped	8 celery stalks, chopped
6 juniper berries	2 tbsp all-purpose flour
2 fresh thyme sprigs, plus	⅔ cup heavy cream
extra to garnish	freshly cooked peas, to serve

cook's tip

Remove the rind from the rolled loin of pork and trim off any visible fat, if necessary, before re-rolling and tying to prepare for cooking.

1 Heat the oil with half the butter in a heavy-bottomed pan or flameproof casserole. Add the pork and cook over medium heat, turning frequently, for 5–10 minutes, or until browned. Transfer to a plate.

2 Add the shallots to the pan and cook, stirring frequently, for 5 minutes, or until softened. Add the juniper berries and thyme sprigs and return the pork to the pan, with any juices that have collected on the plate. Pour in the cider and Stock, season to taste with salt and pepper, then cover and simmer for 30 minutes. Turn the pork over and add the celery. Re-cover the pan and cook for an additional 40 minutes.

3 Meanwhile, make a beurre manié by mashing the remaining butter with the flour in a small bowl. Transfer the pork and celery to a platter with a perforated spoon and keep warm. Remove and discard the juniper berries and thyme. Whisk the beurre manié, a little at a time, into the simmering cooking liquid. Cook, stirring constantly, for 2 minutes, then stir in the cream and bring to a boil. Slice the pork and spoon a little of the sauce over it. Garnish with thyme sprigs and serve immediately with the celery and freshly cooked peas. Hand the remaining sauce separately.

pork with red cabbage

serves 4 | **prep: 20 mins** ⏱ | **cook: 2 hrs** ⏱

The flavors of pork and red cabbage seem to have been made for each other, and here they are cooked to a melting tenderness with just a hint of fruit, sugar, and spice.

INGREDIENTS

1 tbsp corn oil

1 lb 10 oz/750 g boned and rolled pork loin

1 onion, finely chopped

1 lb 2 oz/500 g red cabbage, thick stems removed and leaves shredded

2 large cooking apples, peeled, cored, and sliced

3 cloves

1 tsp brown sugar

3 tbsp lemon juice, and a thinly pared strip of lemon rind

lemon wedges, to garnish

NUTRITIONAL INFORMATION

Calories	.557
Protein	.38g
Carbohydrate	.16g
Sugars	.14g
Fat	.39g
Saturates	.13g

variation

For a slightly more mellow taste, you can substitute 2–3 large, firm pears, peeled and sliced, for the apples.

cook's tip

Choose a firm, glossy red cabbage for this recipe. It doesn't matter if the outer leaves are bruised, as long as the inner leaves look fresh and blemish-free.

1 Preheat the oven to 325°F/160°C. Heat the oil in a flameproof casserole. Add the pork and cook over medium heat, turning frequently, for 5–10 minutes, until browned. Transfer to a plate.

2 Add the chopped onion to the casserole and cook over low heat, stirring occasionally, for 5 minutes, or until softened. Add the cabbage, in batches, and cook, stirring, for 2 minutes. Transfer each batch (mixed with some onion) into a bowl with a perforated spoon.

3 Add the apple slices, cloves, and sugar to the bowl and mix well, then place about half the mixture in the bottom of the casserole. Top with the pork and add the remaining cabbage mixture. Sprinkle in the lemon juice and add the strip of rind. Cover and cook in the preheated oven for 1½ hours.

4 Transfer the pork to a plate. Transfer the cabbage mixture to the plate with a perforated spoon and keep warm. Bring the cooking juices to a boil over high heat and reduce slightly. Slice the pork and arrange on warmed serving plates, surrounded with the cabbage mixture. Spoon the cooking juices over the meat and serve with wedges of lemon.

pork stir-fry with vegetables

cook: 15 mins

prep: 10 mins

serves 4

variation

This stir-fry tastes just as good made with Chicken Stock (see page 13) instead of the pork stock.

This is a very simple dish which lends itself to almost any combination of vegetables that you have to hand, and makes an easy and nutritious quick lunch or evening meal.

INGREDIENTS

2 tbsp vegetable oil

2 garlic cloves, crushed

½-inch/1-cm piece fresh gingerroot, cut into slivers

12 oz/350 g lean pork fillet, thinly sliced

1 carrot, cut into thin strips

1 red bell pepper, seeded and diced

1 fennel bulb, sliced

1 oz/25 g water chestnuts, halved

generous ¾ cup bean sprouts

2 tbsp Chinese rice wine or dry sherry

1¼ cups pork stock

pinch of dark brown sugar

1 tsp cornstarch

2 tsp water

cook's tip

To make pork stock, follow the recipe for Chicken Stock on page 13, substituting 3 lb/1.3 kg of pork and pork bones for the chicken.

1 Heat the oil in a preheated wok. Add the garlic, gingerroot, and pork and stir-fry over high heat for 1–2 minutes, or until the meat is browned and sealed.

2 Add the carrot strips, bell pepper, fennel, and water chestnuts to the wok and stir-fry for 2–3 minutes, then add the bean sprouts and stir-fry for 1 minute. Remove the pork and vegetables, reserve, and keep warm.

3 Add the Chinese rice wine, stock, and sugar to the wok. Blend the cornstarch with the water to make a smooth paste and stir into the sauce. Bring to a boil, stirring constantly, until thickened and clear.

4 Return the meat and vegetables to the wok and cook for 1–2 minutes, or until heated through and coated with the sauce. Serve immediately.

pork hotchpotch

serves 6　　　　**prep: 15 mins** 🕐　　　　**cook: 1 hr 20 mins** 🕑

This tasty pork and tomato hotchpotch requires nothing more than plenty of fresh crusty bread to mop up the delicious juices, but you could also serve it with fresh salad greens.

INGREDIENTS

⅔ cup all-purpose flour

salt and pepper

3 lb/1.3 kg pork fillet, cut into ¼-inch/5-mm slices

4 tbsp corn oil

2 onions, thinly sliced

2 garlic cloves

14 oz/400 g canned chopped tomatoes

1½ cups dry white wine

1 tbsp torn fresh basil leaves

2 tbsp chopped fresh parsley

fresh parsley sprigs, to garnish

fresh crusty bread, to serve

NUTRITIONAL INFORMATION	
Calories	500
Protein	48g
Carbohydrate	18g
Sugars	5g
Fat	23g
Saturates	6g

variation

Substitute 6 peeled, seeded, and chopped fresh tomatoes for the canned ones, adding them with the wine in Step 2.

1 Spread the flour on a plate and season with salt and pepper. Coat the pork slices in the flour, shaking off any excess. Heat the corn oil in a flameproof casserole. Add the pork slices and cook over medium heat, turning occasionally, for 4–5 minutes, or until browned all over. Transfer the pork to a plate with a perforated spoon.

2 Add the onion slices to the casserole and cook over low heat, stirring occasionally, for 10 minutes, or until golden brown. Finely chop the garlic, add it to the pan, and cook for an additional 2 minutes, then add the tomatoes, wine, and basil, and season to taste with salt and pepper. Cook, stirring frequently, for 3 minutes.

3 Return the pork to the casserole, cover, and simmer gently for 1 hour, or until the meat is tender. Snip in the parsley and serve immediately, garnished with parsley sprigs, with fresh crusty bread.

potato & sausage pan-fry

cook: 35 mins **prep: 15 mins** **serves 4**

This dish is a meal in itself, containing both meat and potatoes cooked in a herby wine gravy. A selection of fresh vegetables may be served with the dish, if you wish.

NUTRITIONAL INFORMATION	
Calories	.688
Protein	.21g
Carbohydrate	.44g
Sugars	.5g
Fat	.46g
Saturates	.19g

INGREDIENTS

1 lb 8 oz/675 g waxy potatoes,
cut into cubes

2 tbsp butter

8 large herb sausages

4 smoked bacon strips

1 onion, cut into fourths

1 zucchini, sliced

⅔ cup dry white wine

1¼ cups Vegetable Stock
(see page 13)

1 tsp Worcestershire sauce

2 tbsp chopped mixed fresh herbs,
plus extra to garnish

salt and pepper

cook's tip

Use different flavors of sausage to vary the dish—there are many different varieties available, such as leek and mustard.

1 Cook the potatoes in a large pan of boiling water for 10 minutes, or until softened. Drain thoroughly and reserve.

2 While the potatoes are cooking, melt the butter in a large skillet. Add the sausages and cook over low heat for 5 minutes, turning to brown all over.

3 Add the bacon, onion, zucchini, and parboiled potatoes to the skillet. Cook for an additional 10 minutes, stirring constantly, and turning the sausages frequently.

4 Stir in the white wine, Stock, Worcestershire sauce, and chopped mixed herbs. Season to taste with salt and pepper and cook the

mixture over low heat for 10 minutes. Taste and adjust the seasoning, if necessary.

5 Transfer the potato and sausage pan-fry to warmed serving plates. Garnish with extra chopped herbs and serve immediately.

basque pork & beans

serves 4　　　　　**prep: 15 mins** ⌁　　　　　**cook: 1 hr 30 mins** ⌁

Beans add texture and nutritional value to any casserole. Dried cannellini beans feature in many Italian, Spanish, French, and Greek stews and casseroles, especially during the winter months.

INGREDIENTS

7 oz/200 g dried cannellini beans, soaked overnight in enough cold water to cover

olive oil, for frying

1 lb 5 oz/600 g boneless leg of pork, cut into 2-inch/5-cm chunks

1 large onion, sliced

3 large garlic cloves, crushed

14 oz/400 g canned chopped tomatoes

2 green bell peppers, seeded and sliced

finely grated rind of 1 large orange

salt and pepper

finely chopped fresh parsley, to garnish

NUTRITIONAL INFORMATION	
Calories	352
Protein	39g
Carbohydrate	24g
Sugars	1g
Fat	12g
Saturates	2g

variation

Add sliced and fried chorizo sausage for a spicier dish. Use leftover beans and bell peppers in a pasta sauce.

cook's tip

Canned, pre-cooked cannellini beans are available from some health food stores and large general food stores. Bear in mind that the can juices may contain extra salt or sugar.

1 Preheat the oven to 350°F/180°C. Drain the beans and place in a large pan with fresh water to cover. Bring to a boil and boil rapidly for 10 minutes. Reduce the heat and simmer for 20 minutes. Drain and reserve.

2 Add enough olive oil to a large, heavy-bottomed skillet to cover the bottom in a very thin layer. Add the pork, in batches, and cook over medium heat, turning, until browned all over. Remove from the pan and reserve. Repeat with the remaining pork.

3 Add more oil to the skillet, if necessary, then add the onion slices and cook over low heat for 3 minutes.

Stir in the garlic and cook for an additional 2 minutes. Return the pork to the skillet.

4 Add the tomatoes and bring to a boil. Reduce the heat, then stir in the bell pepper slices, orange rind, and drained beans. Season to taste with salt and pepper, then transfer the contents of the skillet to a large casserole.

Cover the casserole and cook in the preheated oven for 45 minutes, or until the beans and pork are tender. Serve immediately, straight from the casserole, sprinkled with chopped parsley.

pork & sausage bake

⏱ **cook: 1 hr 20 mins**   ◔ **prep: 15 mins**   **serves 4**

NUTRITIONAL INFORMATION	
Calories 575	
Protein 36g	
Carbohydrate 40g	
Sugars 7g	
Fat 31g	
Saturates 11g	

variation

You can use unsmoked sausages for this casserole, but you should brown them with the pork in Step 1.

This would be a lovely treat for a midweek family supper, and you can take time to relax while it's cooking. It is substantial enough to satisfy even the heartiest appetite.

INGREDIENTS

2 tbsp corn oil

2 tbsp butter

1 lb/450 g pork fillet or loin cut

into thin strips

1 large onion, chopped

1 red bell pepper, seeded and sliced

1 orange bell pepper, seeded and sliced

4 oz/115 g mushrooms, sliced

scant ¾ cup long-grain rice

generous 1¾ cups Beef Stock

(see page 13)

8 oz/225 g smoked sausage, sliced

¼ tsp ground allspice

salt and pepper

2 tbsp chopped fresh parsley,

to garnish

cook's tip

A huge variety of smoked sausages are available, from pepperoni and many types of salami to *saucisson fume aux herbes*, with a herb coating.

1 Preheat the oven to 350°F/180°C. Heat the oil and butter in a large, flameproof casserole. Add the pork and cook over medium heat, stirring, for 5 minutes, until browned. Transfer to a plate.

2 Add the onion and cook over low heat, stirring occasionally, for 5 minutes, or until softened. Add the bell peppers and cook, stirring frequently, for an additional 4–5 minutes. Add the mushrooms and cook for 1 minute, then stir in the rice. Cook for 1 minute, or until the grains are well coated, then add the Stock and bring to a boil.

3 Return the pork to the casserole, add the sausage and allspice, and season to taste with salt and pepper. Mix thoroughly, cover, and cook in the preheated oven for 1 hour, or until all the liquid has been absorbed and the meat is tender. Serve immediately, garnished with chopped parsley.

spicy sausage with lentils

serves 4　　　　**prep: 10 mins** ◔　　　　**cook: 25 mins** ◷

A cross between a soup and a stew, this filling dish can be made with almost anything lurking in the pantry and refrigerator, so if you are short of one or two ingredients, be creative!

INGREDIENTS

1 tbsp corn oil

8 oz/225 g spicy sausages, sliced

4 oz/115 g rindless smoked
bacon, chopped

1 onion, chopped

6 tbsp strained tomatoes

generous 1¾ cups Beef Stock
(see page 13)

1 lb 5 oz/600 g canned lentils,
drained and rinsed

½ tsp paprika

2 tsp red wine vinegar

salt and pepper

fresh thyme sprigs, to garnish

NUTRITIONAL INFORMATION

Calories	428
Protein	. . . . .23g
Carbohydrate	. . . . .23g
Sugars	. . . . .5g
Fat	. . . . .28g
Saturates	. . . . .10g

variation

You can substitute other canned pulses for the lentils, and to turn this into a fish dish, use smoked mackerel instead of the sausages.

1 Heat the oil in a large, heavy-bottomed pan. Add the sausages and bacon and cook over medium heat, stirring, for 5 minutes, or until the bacon begins to crisp. Transfer to a plate with a perforated spoon.

2 Add the chopped onion to the pan and cook, stirring occasionally, for 5 minutes, or until softened. Stir in the strained tomatoes and add the Stock and lentils. Reduce the heat, cover, and simmer for 10 minutes.

3 Return the sausage slices and bacon to the pan, stir in the paprika and red wine vinegar, and season to taste with salt and pepper. Heat the mixture through gently for a few minutes, then serve immediately, garnished with fresh thyme sprigs.

leek & sausage tortilla

⏲ **cook: 15 mins**   ◔ **prep: 5 mins**   **serves 2**

Serve this tasty Spanish omelet-style dish with salad greens
for a nourishing and tasty supper or a delicious light lunch.
It is incredibly easy and quick to put together.

NUTRITIONAL INFORMATION

Calories 540

Protein 33g

Carbohydrate 10g

Sugars 9g

Fat 42g

Saturates 12g

INGREDIENTS

4 oz/115 g chorizo sausage

2 tbsp olive oil

4 leeks, thinly sliced

½ red bell pepper, seeded and chopped

6 eggs

salt and pepper

variation

If you like, sprinkle the cooked tortilla with ½ cup of grated Cheddar cheese while still in the pan and brown under a medium broiler for 2 minutes.

1 Slice the sausage. Heat the oil in a large skillet. Add the leeks and cook over medium heat, stirring occasionally, for 5 minutes, or until softened. Add the bell pepper and sausage slices and cook for 5 minutes.

2 Beat the eggs in a bowl and season to taste with salt and pepper. Pour the eggs into the skillet and cook for a few seconds. Loosen any egg that has set at the edge of the pan with a spatula and tilt the pan to let the uncooked egg run underneath. Continue cooking until the underside has set.

3 Remove the skillet from the heat, place an upside-down plate on top and, holding the 2 together, invert the tortilla on to the plate. Slide it back into the skillet and cook for an additional 2 minutes, until the second side has set. Slide the tortilla out of the skillet and cut into wedges to serve.

brunswick stew

serves 6 **prep: 15 mins** **cook: 1 hr 20 mins**

This traditional chicken stew is a hearty dish, which is suffused with warm, spicy undertones. Serve it with salad and whole-wheat bread rolls to make a filling, warming winter supper.

INGREDIENTS

4 lb/1.8 kg chicken pieces

salt

2 tbsp paprika

2 tbsp olive oil

2 tbsp butter

1 lb/450 g onions, chopped

2 yellow bell peppers, seeded and chopped

14 oz/400 g canned chopped tomatoes

scant 1 cup dry white wine

generous 1¾ cups Chicken Stock (see page 13)

1 tbsp Worcestershire sauce

½ tsp Tabasco sauce

1 tbsp finely chopped fresh parsley

11½ oz/325 g canned corn kernels, drained

15 oz/425 g canned lima beans, drained and rinsed

2 tbsp all-purpose flour

4 tbsp water

fresh parsley sprigs, to garnish

NUTRITIONAL INFORMATION	
Calories	.670
Protein	.46g
Carbohydrate	.37g
Sugars	.14g
Fat	.36g
Saturates	.11g

variation

If you don't have time to make a chicken stock for this dish, use water instead, which works almost as well.

cook's tip

If you decide to substitute fresh tomatoes for canned tomatoes in a stew, add 1 tablespoon of tomato paste to the dish at the same time, to make sure that the flavor is strong enough.

1 Season the chicken pieces with salt and dust with paprika.

2 Heat the oil and butter in a flameproof casserole or large pan. Add the chicken pieces and cook over medium heat, turning, for 10–15 minutes, or until golden. Transfer to a plate with a perforated spoon.

3 Add the onion and bell peppers to the casserole. Cook over low heat, stirring occasionally, for 5 minutes, or until softened. Add the tomatoes, wine, Stock, Worcestershire sauce, Tabasco sauce, and parsley and bring to a boil, stirring. Return the chicken to the casserole, cover, and simmer, stirring occasionally, for 30 minutes.

4 Add the corn and beans to the casserole, partially re-cover, and simmer for an additional 30 minutes. Place the flour and water in a small bowl and mix to make a paste. Stir a ladleful of the cooking liquid into the paste, then stir it into the stew. Cook, stirring frequently, for 5 minutes. Serve, garnished with parsley.

provençal chicken

cook: 1 hr　　　　**prep: 20 mins**　　　　**serves 4**

NUTRITIONAL INFORMATION

Calories 770

Protein 60g

Carbohydrate 9g

Sugars 4g

Fat 52g

Saturates 13g

variation

If you would like a little extra garlic in this dish, crush another clove into the casserole with the stock in Step 2.

This colorful dish incorporates all the wonderful flavors of southern France—olives, garlic, anchovies, tomatoes, olive oil, and oregano.

INGREDIENTS

4 lb/1.8 kg chicken pieces

salt and pepper

1 garlic clove, finely chopped

3 tbsp olive oil

1 onion, finely chopped

8 oz/225 g mushrooms, halved

1 tbsp all-purpose flour

½ cup Chicken Stock (see page 13)

¾ cup dry white wine

6 canned anchovy fillets, drained

3 tomatoes, peeled, seeded and chopped

2 tsp chopped fresh oregano

6 black olives, pitted

cook's tip

Test that chicken is cooked through by piercing the thickest part with the point of a sharp knife. If the juices run clear, the chicken is ready, but if there is any trace of pink, cook for a little longer.

1 Rub the chicken pieces all over with salt, pepper, and garlic. Heat the oil in a flameproof casserole. Add the chicken and cook over medium heat, turning occasionally, for 8–10 minutes, or until golden. Add the onion, cover, and cook over low heat, stirring occasionally, for 20–25 minutes, or until cooked through and tender.

2 Transfer the chicken to a large serving plate, cover, and keep warm. Add the mushrooms to the casserole and cook over medium heat, stirring constantly, for 3 minutes. Add the flour and cook, stirring constantly, for 1 minute, then gradually stir in the Stock and wine. Bring to a boil and cook, stirring, for 10 minutes, or until thickened.

3 Coarsely chop 4 of the anchovies and add them to the casserole with the tomatoes, oregano, and olives, then simmer for 5 minutes. Meanwhile, cut the remaining anchovies in half lengthwise. Transfer the sauce and chicken to serving plates, garnish with the halved anchovies, and serve immediately.

coq au vin

serves 4   **prep: 20 mins**   **cook: 1 hr 15 mins**

Traditional recipes often yield wonderfully tasty results, and this dish is no exception. Serve this perennial favorite with warm French bread or garlic bread to mop up the delicious wine-flavored juices.

INGREDIENTS

¼ cup butter

2 tbsp olive oil

4 lb/1.8 kg chicken pieces

4 oz/115 g rindless smoked bacon, cut into strips

4 oz/115 g pearl onions

4 oz/115 g cremini mushrooms, halved

2 garlic cloves, finely chopped

2 tbsp brandy

scant 1 cup red wine

1¼ cups Chicken Stock (see page 13)

1 bouquet garni

salt and pepper

2 tbsp all-purpose flour

bay leaves, to garnish

NUTRITIONAL INFORMATION	
Calories	.966
Protein	.62g
Carbohydrate	.11g
Sugars	.2g
Fat	.69g
Saturates	.24g

variation

You can substitute a good, full-bodied white wine such as Chardonnay for the red wine, if you prefer.

cook's tip

If you like, cook the chicken in the oven instead of on the hob. Transfer it to a preheated oven, 325°F/160°C, once the mixture has come to a boil in Step 2. Cook for 1 hour, then follow Step 3.

1 Melt half the butter with the olive oil in a large, flameproof casserole. Add the chicken and cook over medium heat, stirring, for 8–10 minutes, or until golden brown. Add the bacon, onions, mushrooms, and garlic.

2 Pour in the brandy and set it alight with a match or taper. When the flames have died down, add the wine, Stock, and bouquet garni and season to taste with salt and pepper. Bring to a boil, reduce the heat, and simmer gently for 1 hour, or until the chicken pieces are cooked through and tender. Meanwhile, make a beurre manié by mashing the remaining butter with the flour in a small bowl.

3 Remove and discard the bouquet garni. Transfer the chicken to a large plate and keep warm. Stir the beurre manié into the casserole, a little at a time. Bring to a boil, return the chicken to the casserole, and serve immediately, garnished with bay leaves.

chicken bonne femme

serves 4　　　　**prep: 15 mins** ⏱　　　　**cook: 1 hr 15 mins** ♨

Bonne femme, meaning "good woman," describes simple, rustic French dishes that are often served straight from the cooking dish. Chicken Bonne Femme is probably the most famous recipe.

INGREDIENTS

4 lb/1.8 kg oven-ready chicken

salt and pepper

¼ cup unsalted butter

1 lb 8 oz/675 g pearl onions

1 lb 8 oz/675 g new potatoes

6 rindless bacon strips, diced

1 bouquet garni

NUTRITIONAL INFORMATION

Calories 1029

Protein 66g

Carbohydrate 41g

Sugars 12g

Fat 68g

Saturates 25g

1 Preheat the oven to 350°F/180°C. Rinse the chicken inside and out, then pat dry with paper towels. Season well with salt and pepper. Melt the butter in a flameproof casserole. Add the chicken and cook over medium heat, turning frequently, for 8–10 minutes, or until golden. Transfer to a plate.

2 Add the pearl onions, potatoes, and bacon to the casserole and cook over low heat, stirring occasionally, until the onions soften and the potatoes begin to color.

3 Return the chicken to the casserole and add the bouquet garni. Cover and cook in the preheated oven for about 1 hour, or until the

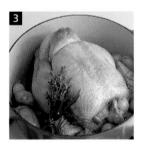

chicken is cooked through and tender. Remove and discard the bouquet garni. Transfer the chicken to a large serving platter, surround it with the vegetables and bacon, and serve immediately.

cook's tip

If you are serving this meal at a dinner party or special lunch, give the finished dish a regal look by stuffing the neck of the cooked chicken with fresh thyme and bay sprigs.

chicken cacciatore

cook: 1 hr 20 mins   **prep: 15 mins**   **serves 4**

Cacciatore refers to the Italian term "alla cacciatora," meaning "hunter's-style." This recipe follows that tradition, and is a rich and filling dish designed to give warmth and energy.

NUTRITIONAL INFORMATION

Calories 406

Protein 39g

Carbohydrate 10g

Sugars 7g

Fat 21g

Saturates 5g

INGREDIENTS

3 tbsp olive oil

4 lb/1.8 kg skinless chicken pieces

2 red onions, sliced

2 garlic cloves, finely chopped

14 oz/400 g canned chopped tomatoes

2 tbsp chopped fresh flatleaf parsley

1 tbsp sun-dried tomato paste

⅔ cup red wine

6 fresh basil leaves

salt and pepper

fresh basil sprigs, to garnish

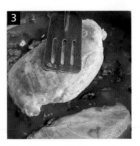

cook's tip

To make this casserole an even more substantial meal, serve it with freshly cooked tagliatelle or penne, or with an Italian-style olive and tomato salad.

1 Preheat the oven to 325°F/160°C. Heat the olive oil in a flameproof casserole. Add the chicken and cook over medium heat, stirring frequently, for 5–10 minutes, or until golden. Transfer to a plate with a perforated spoon.

2 Add the onions and garlic to the casserole and cook over low heat, stirring occasionally, for 10 minutes, or until golden. Add the tomatoes and their juices, the parsley, tomato paste, and wine, and tear in the basil leaves. Season to taste with salt and pepper.

3 Bring the mixture to a boil, then return the chicken to the casserole, pushing it down into the cooking liquid. Cover and cook in the preheated oven for 1 hour, or until the chicken is cooked through and tender. Serve immediately, garnished with fresh basil sprigs.

louisiana chicken

serves 4   **prep: 20 mins** ⟳   **cook: 1 hr 15 mins** ⟳

*You can make this colorful American dish as mild or as spicy
as you like by varying the quantity of chopped fresh chiles,
or by adding a dash of hot Tabasco sauce before serving.*

INGREDIENTS

5 tbsp corn oil	**2 fresh red chiles, seeded**
4 chicken portions	**and finely chopped**
6 tbsp all-purpose flour	**14 oz/400 g canned chopped tomatoes**
1 onion, chopped	**1¼ cups Chicken Stock (see page 13)**
2 celery stalks, sliced	**salt and pepper**
1 green bell pepper, seeded	
and chopped	**GARNISH**
2 garlic cloves, finely chopped	**corn salad**
2 tsp chopped fresh thyme	**chopped fresh thyme**

NUTRITIONAL INFORMATION

Calories	573
Protein	38g
Carbohydrate	18g
Sugars	6g
Fat	40g
Saturates	9g

variation

Substitute shrimp or crayfish for the
chicken. If raw, cook until they change
color in Step 1 and return to the
casserole near the end to heat through.

cook's tip

The success of this dish
depends on the roux (the flour
and fat mixture) reaching the
right stage in Step 2. It should
be the color of peanut butter.
Don't try to hurry the process,
or the flour will burn.

1 Heat the oil in a large,
heavy-bottomed pan
or flameproof casserole. Add
the chicken and cook over
medium heat, stirring, for
5–10 minutes, or until golden.
Transfer the chicken to a plate
with a perforated spoon.

2 Stir the flour into the
oil and cook over very
low heat, stirring constantly,

for 15 minutes, or until light
golden. Do not let it burn.
Immediately, add the onion,
celery, and green bell pepper
and cook, stirring constantly,
for 2 minutes. Add the garlic,
thyme, and chiles and cook,
stirring, for 1 minute.

3 Stir in the tomatoes
and their juices, then
gradually stir in the Stock.

Return the chicken pieces
to the pan, cover, and simmer
for 45 minutes, or until the
chicken is cooked through and
tender. Season to taste with
salt and pepper, transfer to
warmed serving plates and
serve immediately, garnished
with some corn salad and a
sprinkling of chopped thyme.

chicken in white wine

⏱ **cook: 1 hr 50 mins**   ⏲ **prep: 20 mins**   **serves 4**

NUTRITIONAL INFORMATION

Calories	.894
Protein	.60g
Carbohydrate	.8g
Sugars	.2g
Fat	.63g
Saturates	.21g

Not so well known as its cousin Coq au Vin (see page 100), where chicken is cooked in red wine, this is nevertheless a popular classic and just as tasty. Serve with rice or potatoes.

INGREDIENTS

2 thick, rindless, lean bacon strips

¼ cup butter

2 tbsp olive oil

4 oz/115 g pearl onions

1 garlic clove, finely chopped

4 lb/1.8 kg chicken pieces

1¾ cups dry white wine

1¼ cups Chicken Stock

(see page 13)

1 bouquet garni

salt and pepper

4 oz/115 g white mushrooms

2½ tbsp all-purpose flour

fresh mixed herbs, to garnish

variation

If you prefer, replace the bouquet garni with 1 small bunch of fresh thyme and garnish the finished dish with chopped fresh flatleaf parsley instead of the mixed herbs.

cook's tip

If there is not much room for you to stir in Step 3, transfer the chicken to serving plates and keep warm while you whisk the beurre manié into the sauce. Spoon the sauce over the chicken to serve.

1 Preheat the oven to 325°F/160°C. Chop the bacon. Melt half the butter with the oil in a flameproof casserole. Add the bacon and cook over medium heat, stirring, for 5–10 minutes, or until golden brown. Transfer the bacon to a large plate. Add the onions and garlic to the casserole and cook over low heat, stirring occasionally, for 10 minutes, or until golden. Transfer to the plate. Add the chicken and cook over medium heat, stirring constantly, for 8–10 minutes, or until golden. Transfer to the plate.

2 Drain off any excess fat from the casserole. Stir in the wine and Stock and bring to a boil, scraping any sediment off the bottom. Add the bouquet garni and season to taste. Return the bacon, onions, and chicken to the casserole. Cover and cook in the preheated oven for 1 hour. Add the white mushrooms, re-cover, and cook for 15 minutes. Meanwhile, make a beurre manié by mashing the remaining butter with the flour in a small bowl.

3 Remove the casserole from the oven and set over medium heat. Remove and discard the bouquet garni. Whisk in the beurre manié, a little at a time. Bring to a boil, stirring constantly, then serve, garnished with fresh herb sprigs.

red hot chili chicken

cook: 40 mins   **prep: 20 mins**   **serves 4**

NUTRITIONAL INFORMATION	
Calories	290
Protein	36g
Carbohydrate	10g
Sugars	8g
Fat	12g
Saturates	3g

This is a really fiery curry with a wonderfully aromatic, home-made chili paste, for those who like it hot. You can mix the spice paste by hand with a pestle and mortar if you have to, but it is much quicker and easier to use a blender or food processor.

variation

If you prefer a milder version of this dish, try to find Ancho or Anaheim varieties of chiles and seed them before using.

INGREDIENTS

1 tbsp curry paste
2 fresh green chiles, chopped
5 dried red chiles
2 tbsp tomato paste
2 garlic cloves, chopped
1 tsp chili powder
pinch of sugar
pinch of salt
2 tbsp peanut or corn oil
½ tsp cumin seeds
1 onion, chopped
2 curry leaves

1 tsp ground cumin
1 tsp ground coriander
½ tsp ground turmeric
14 oz/400 g canned chopped tomatoes
⅔ cup Chicken Stock (see page 13)
4 skinless, boneless chicken breasts
1 tsp garam masala

TO SERVE
freshly cooked rice
plain yogurt

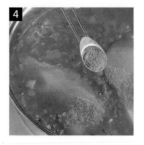

cook's tip

Indian cooks usually make their own garam masala, but it is available ready-made from major food stores and specialist Indian stores.

1 To make the chili paste, place the curry paste, fresh and dried chiles, tomato paste, garlic, chili powder, and sugar in a blender or food processor with the salt. Process to a smooth paste.

2 Heat the oil in a large, heavy-bottomed pan. Add the cumin seeds and cook over medium heat, stirring constantly, for 2 minutes, or until they begin to pop and release their aroma. Add the onion and curry leaves and cook, stirring, for 5 minutes.

3 Add the chili paste, cook for 2 minutes, then stir in the ground cumin, coriander, and turmeric and cook for an additional 2 minutes.

4 Add the tomatoes and their juices and the Stock. Bring to a boil, then reduce the heat and simmer for 5 minutes. Add the chicken and garam masala, cover, and simmer gently for 20 minutes, or until the chicken is cooked through and tender. Serve immediately with freshly cooked rice and yogurt.

chicken jalfrezi

serves 4 **prep: 15 mins** (ᴸ **cook: 30 mins** (⏲

*This is a quick and tasty way to use leftover roast chicken. The
sauce can also be used for any cooked poultry, lamb, or beef.*

INGREDIENTS

½ tsp cumin seeds	½ tsp garam masala
½ tsp coriander seeds	1 tsp red wine vinegar
1 tsp mustard oil	1 small red bell pepper, chopped
3 tbsp vegetable oil	4½ oz/125 g frozen fava beans
1 large onion, finely chopped	1 lb 2 oz/500 g cooked chicken,
3 garlic cloves, crushed	chopped
1 tbsp tomato paste	salt
2 tomatoes, peeled and chopped	fresh cilantro sprigs, to garnish
1 tsp ground turmeric	freshly cooked rice, to serve
½ tsp chili powder	

variation

When in season, use fresh, shelled
fava beans and if time is limited, use
ground cumin and coriander instead
of grinding the seeds yourself.

cook's tip

Chunks of lean cooked turkey
or pork also go well with this
combination of flavors. With
both meats, the cooking time
remains the same.

1 Grind the cumin and
coriander seeds in a
mortar with a pestle, then
reserve. Heat the mustard oil
in a large, heavy-bottomed
skillet over high heat for
1 minute, or until it begins to
smoke. Add the vegetable oil,
reduce the heat, and add the
onion and garlic. Cook for
10 minutes, or until golden.

2 Add the tomato paste,
chopped tomatoes,
turmeric, ground cumin and
coriander seeds, chili powder,
garam masala, and vinegar
to the skillet. Stir the mixture
until fragrant.

3 Add the red bell pepper
and fava beans and
stir for an additional 2 minutes,
or until the bell pepper is
softened. Stir in the chicken,
and season to taste with
salt, then simmer gently for
6–8 minutes, until the chicken
is heated through and the
beans are tender. Transfer to
warmed serving plates, garnish
with cilantro sprigs, and serve
with freshly cooked rice.

chicken pasanda

serves 4

prep: 20 mins, ⏱
plus 2–3 hrs marinating

cook: 25 mins ⏱

This Balti dish is traditionally cooked and served in a karahi—a pan similar in shape to a wok. If you have neither a karahi nor a wok, use a large, heavy-bottomed skillet instead.

INGREDIENTS

4 cardamom pods	1 lb 8 oz/675 g skinless, boneless
6 black peppercorns	chicken, diced
½ cinnamon stick	5 tbsp peanut oil
½ tsp cumin seeds	2 onions, finely chopped
2 tsp garam masala	3 fresh green chiles, seeded
1 tsp chili powder	and chopped
1 tsp grated fresh gingerroot	2 tbsp chopped fresh cilantro
1 garlic clove, very finely chopped	½ cup light cream
4 tbsp thick plain yogurt	fresh cilantro sprigs, to garnish
pinch of salt	

NUTRITIONAL INFORMATION

Calories	.426
Protein	.41g
Carbohydrate	.8g
Sugars	.7g
Fat	.26g
Saturates	.7g

variation

If you cannot find any peanut oil at your local food store, you can substitute corn oil instead.

cook's tip

When this is served in the traditional way, all the diners tear off pieces of naan bread and scoop out some of the mixture from the karahi.

1 Place the cardamom pods in a nonmetallic dish with the peppercorns, cinnamon, cumin, garam masala, chili powder, gingerroot, garlic, yogurt, and salt. Add the chicken pieces and stir well to coat. Cover and let marinate in the refrigerator for 2–3 hours.

2 Heat the oil in a preheated wok or karahi. Add the onions and cook over low heat, stirring occasionally, for 5 minutes, or until softened, then add the chicken pieces and marinade and cook over medium heat, stirring, for 15 minutes, or until the chicken is cooked through.

3 Stir in the fresh chiles and cilantro and pour in the cream. Heat through gently, but do not let it boil. Garnish with fresh cilantro and serve immediately.

mexican turkey

cook: 1 hr 10 mins   **prep: 15 mins**   **serves 4**

Using chocolate in savory dishes is a Mexican tradition and, while it may sound strange, it gives the meat a very rich flavor. Mexican chocolate often has cinnamon incorporated into it, but you can use ordinary semisweet chocolate and ground cinnamon for this dish.

INGREDIENTS

6 tbsp all-purpose flour	4 tomatoes, peeled, seeded,
salt and pepper	and chopped
4 turkey breast fillets	1 tsp chili powder
3 tbsp corn oil	½ tsp ground cinnamon
1 onion, thinly sliced	pinch of ground cumin
1 red bell pepper, seeded and sliced	1 oz/25 g semisweet chocolate, finely
1¼ cups Chicken Stock	chopped or grated
(see page 13)	chopped fresh cilantro, to garnish
2 tbsp raisins	

variation

You can also prepare this dish with 1 lb 8 oz/675 g of diced, lean beef, but you will need to allow an extra 15 minutes cooking time.

cook's tip

For the best flavor, choose the best quality chocolate you can find for this dish. It should contain a minimum of 70 percent cocoa solids.

1 Preheat the oven to 325°F/160°C. Spread the flour on a plate and season with salt and pepper. Coat the turkey fillets in the seasoned flour, shaking off any excess.

2 Heat the oil in a flameproof casserole. Add the turkey fillets and cook over medium heat, turning occasionally, for 5–10 minutes, or until golden. Transfer to a plate with a perforated spoon.

3 Add the onion and bell pepper to the casserole. Cook over low heat, stirring occasionally, for 5 minutes, or until softened. Sprinkle in any remaining seasoned flour and cook, stirring constantly, for 1 minute. Gradually stir in the Stock, then add the raisins, chopped tomatoes, chili powder, cinnamon, cumin, and chocolate. Season to taste with salt and pepper. Bring to a boil, stirring constantly.

4 Return the turkey to the casserole, cover, and cook in the preheated oven for 50 minutes. Serve immediately, garnished with cilantro.

italian turkey steaks

serves 4   **prep: 10 mins**   **cook: 50 mins**

This lively summer dish is simplicity itself, but tastes really wonderful and makes a surprisingly substantial main course.

INGREDIENTS

1 tbsp olive oil

4 turkey scallops or steaks

2 red bell peppers

1 red onion

2 garlic cloves, finely chopped

1¼ cups strained tomatoes

⅔ cup medium white wine

1 tbsp chopped fresh marjoram

salt and pepper

14 oz/400 g canned cannellini beans, drained and rinsed

3 tbsp fresh white bread crumbs

fresh basil sprigs, to garnish

NUTRITIONAL INFORMATION	
Calories	.264
Protein	.33g
Carbohydrate	.18g
Sugars	.11g
Fat	.5g
Saturates	.1g

variation

Soak ½ oz/15 g of dried porcini mushrooms in boiling water to cover for 20 minutes. Drain and slice, then add with the onion and bell peppers in Step 2.

1 Heat the oil in a flameproof casserole or heavy-bottomed skillet. Add the turkey scallops and cook over medium heat for 5–10 minutes, turning occasionally, until golden. Transfer to a plate.

2 Seed and slice the red bell peppers. Slice the onion, add to the skillet with the bell peppers, and cook over low heat, stirring occasionally, for 5 minutes, or until softened. Add the garlic and cook for an additional 2 minutes. Return the turkey to the skillet and add the strained tomatoes, wine, and marjoram. Season to taste. Bring to a boil, then reduce the heat, cover, and simmer, stirring occasionally, for 25–30 minutes, or until the turkey is cooked through and tender.

3 Stir in the cannellini beans. Simmer for an additional 5 minutes. Sprinkle the bread crumbs over the top and place under a preheated medium–hot broiler for 2–3 minutes, or until golden. Serve, garnished with basil.

turkey in a piquant sauce

cook: 1 hr 45 mins   **prep: 20 mins**   serves 4

Turkey portions make an easy and economical family supper. Here they are served in a delicious tomato and bell pepper sauce.

NUTRITIONAL INFORMATION	
Calories	290
Protein	29g
Carbohydrate	13g
Sugars	6g
Fat	14g
Saturates	5g

INGREDIENTS

2 tbsp all-purpose flour

salt and pepper

2 lb 4 oz/1 kg turkey pieces

2 tbsp butter

1 tbsp corn oil

2 onions, sliced

1 garlic clove, finely chopped

1 red bell pepper, seeded and sliced

14 oz/400 g canned chopped tomatoes

1 sprig rosemary

⅔ cup Chicken Stock (see page 13)

2 tbsp chopped fresh parsley,
to garnish

variation

This recipe also works just as well with chicken pieces. Chicken is more tender than turkey, so reduce the simmering time at the end of Step 3 to 45 minutes.

1 Spread the flour on a plate and season with salt and pepper. Coat the turkey pieces in the seasoned flour, shaking off any excess.

2 Melt the butter with the oil in a flameproof casserole or large pan. Add the turkey and cook over medium heat, stirring, for 5–10 minutes, or until golden.

Transfer the turkey pieces to a plate with a perforated spoon and keep warm.

3 Add the onions, garlic, and bell pepper to the casserole and cook, stirring occasionally, for 5 minutes, or until softened. Sprinkle in any remaining flour and cook, stirring constantly, for 1 minute. Return the turkey pieces to the

casserole, then add the tomatoes and their juices, the rosemary, and Stock. Bring to a boil, stirring constantly, then cover and simmer for 1¼ hours, or until the turkey is cooked through and tender.

4 Transfer the turkey to a serving platter with a perforated spoon. Remove and discard the rosemary.

Return the sauce to a boil and cook until reduced and thickened. Season to taste with salt and pepper and pour over the turkey. Serve immediately, garnished with parsley.

fish & seafood

The range of seafood available these days is immense, but sometimes it is difficult to know how to cook unfamiliar fish. The answer might be to put it into a pot and make a fabulous stew—Fishermen's Stew (see page 122) is incredibly easy to make and equally delicious.

This section is packed with recipes with an international flavor, from Chinese Sweet & Sour Shrimp (see page 148), Thai Shrimp Curry (see page 147), and the Swedish casserole Jansson's Temptation (see page 135) to Mediterranean delights, such as Swordfish with Tomatoes & Olives (see page 126). A little sophistication is also introduced in the traditional French dish, Moules Marinières (see page 143).

The following pages include ideas for preparing every kind of seafood, from shrimp and tuna to monkfish and squid—and not an unhealthy chip in sight. Whether you are looking for a hot curry, a warming casserole, or a traditional paella, you are bound to find a meal to suit every occasion.

cod in lemon & parsley

cook: 25 mins   **prep: 15 mins**   **serves 4**

NUTRITIONAL INFORMATION	
Calories 248	
Protein 34g	
Carbohydrate 9g	
Sugars 7g	
Fat 7g	
Saturates 1g	

This is a very simple way to cook fish, with lovely, refreshing, Mediterranean flavors. Any firm white fish steaks or fillets are equally good at absorbing the flavors of this delicious dish.

INGREDIENTS

2 onions	6 tbsp dry white wine
1 garlic clove	3 tbsp chopped fresh mixed herbs,
2 tbsp olive oil	such as parsley, thyme, and chives
4 tomatoes, peeled and	4 cod steaks, about 6 oz/175 g each
cut into fourths	salt and pepper
grated rind and juice of ½ lemon	fresh thyme sprigs, to garnish

variation

If you want to substitute another white fish for the cod, try firm steaks of whiting, halibut, or haddock.

cook's tip

This is an excellent emergency dish to have on standby when you have unexpected visitors, and it tastes just as good made with frozen fish. Thaw under cold—not hot—water, or in the microwave before cooking.

1 Finely chop the onions and garlic. Heat the olive oil in a large, heavy-bottomed skillet. Add the onion and cook over low heat, stirring occasionally, for 5 minutes, or until softened.

2 Add the garlic and tomatoes and cook for 3–4 minutes. Add the lemon rind and juice, white wine, chopped herbs, and cod steaks, and season to taste with salt and pepper.

3 Set the heat as low as possible, then cover the skillet and simmer gently for 15 minutes, or until the fish is cooked through and flakes easily when tested with the point of a knife. Serve immediately, garnished with fresh thyme sprigs.

fishermen's stew

serves 6   **prep: 20 mins**   **cook: 35 mins**

This richly flavored mixture of fish and shellfish is a fabulous way to feed guests, as it is easy to prepare and needs no more accompaniment than chunks of fresh bread or crusty rolls.

INGREDIENTS

3 lb 5 oz/1.5 kg live mussels
3 tbsp olive oil
2 onions, chopped
3 garlic cloves, finely chopped
1 red bell pepper, seeded and sliced
3 carrots, chopped
1 lb 12 oz/800 g canned chopped tomatoes
½ cup dry white wine
2 tbsp tomato paste
1 tbsp chopped fresh dill

2 tbsp chopped fresh parsley
1 tbsp chopped fresh thyme
1 tbsp fresh basil leaves, plus extra to garnish
2 lb/900 g white fish fillets, cut into chunks
1 lb/450 g raw shrimp
1½ cups Fish Stock (see page 13) or water
salt and pepper

NUTRITIONAL INFORMATION	
Calories	340
Protein	49g
Carbohydrate	14g
Sugars	12g
Fat	9g
Saturates	1g

variation

If you can't find raw shrimp, use cooked ones and add them for the last 2–3 minutes of the cooking time in Step 3. They need only heat through.

cook's tip

When you buy live mussels, make sure that the shells are pristine, not cracked or broken. Always prepare them carefully, following the instructions in Steps 1 and 4.

1 Clean the mussels by scrubbing or scraping the shells and pulling off any beards. Discard any with broken shells or any that refuse to close when tapped with a knife. Rinse the mussels under cold running water.

2 Heat the oil in a flameproof casserole. Add the onions, garlic, bell pepper, and carrots and cook over low heat, stirring occasionally, for 5 minutes, or until softened.

3 Add the tomatoes and their juices, the white wine, tomato paste, dill, parsley, and thyme, and tear in the basil leaves. Bring to a boil, then reduce the heat and simmer for 20 minutes.

4 Add the chunks of fish, mussels, shrimp, and Stock and season to taste with salt and pepper. Return the stew to a boil and simmer for 6–8 minutes, or until the shrimp have turned pink and the mussel shells have opened. Discard any shells that remain closed. Serve immediately, garnished with basil leaves.

mediterranean fish stew

⏲ **cook: 30 mins**   ⏱ **prep: 20 mins**   **serves 4**

NUTRITIONAL INFORMATION

Calories	.377
Protein	.51g
Carbohydrate	.13g
Sugars	.8g
Fat	.10g
Saturates	.1g

Serve this aromatic stew in bowls or shallow soup plates, with spoons as well as forks, to ensure that everyone has plenty of the delicious tomato-and-saffron-flavored broth.

INGREDIENTS

2 tbsp olive oil	¾ cup dry white wine
1 onion, sliced	12 oz/350 g red snapper or pompano
pinch of saffron threads,	fillets, cut into chunks
lightly crushed	1 lb/450 g angler fish fillet,
1 tbsp chopped fresh thyme	cut into chunks
salt and pepper	1 lb/450 g fresh clams
2 garlic cloves, finely chopped	8 oz/225 g squid rings
1 lb 12 oz/800 g canned chopped	2 tbsp fresh basil leaves, plus
tomatoes, drained	extra to garnish
8 cups Fish Stock (see page 13)	

variation

If you can't find clams, use mussels. Follow the instructions in the Cook's Tip on page 122, and make sure the shells have opened before serving.

cook's tip

Although saffron is very expensive, it has a unique flavor that is worth including in this stew and, in any case, you use only a small quantity.

1 Heat the oil in a large, flameproof casserole. Add the onion, saffron, thyme, and a pinch of salt. Cook over low heat, stirring occasionally, for 5 minutes, or until the onion has softened.

2 Add the garlic and cook for an additional 2 minutes, then add the drained tomatoes and pour in the Stock and wine. Season to taste with salt and pepper, bring the mixture to a boil, then reduce the heat and simmer for 15 minutes.

3 Add the chunks of red snapper and angler fish and simmer for 3 minutes. Add the clams and squid and simmer for 5 minutes, or until the clam shells have opened.

Discard any clams that remain closed. Tear in the basil and stir. Serve garnished with the extra basil leaves.

swordfish with tomatoes & olives

serves 4   **prep: 15 mins** ⟳   **cook: 40 mins** ⟳

Treat your family to this wonderful dish for an alfresco supper. Its flavor is very distinctive, so serve it with a side dish that won't compete—such as straightforward salad greens.

INGREDIENTS

2 tbsp olive oil

1 onion, finely chopped

1 celery stalk, finely chopped

4 oz/115 g green olives, pitted

1 lb/450 g tomatoes, chopped

3 tbsp bottled capers, drained

salt and pepper

4 swordfish steaks,
about 5 oz/140 g each

fresh flatleaf parsley sprigs,
to garnish

NUTRITIONAL INFORMATION	
Calories	.250
Protein	.26g
Carbohydrate	.5g
Sugars	.4g
Fat	.14g
Saturates	.3g

variation

Swordfish is a very firm, meaty fish, but you could substitute cod steaks, monkfish tail, or even shark steaks, if you like.

1 Heat the oil in a large, heavy-bottomed pan. Add the onion and celery and cook over low heat, stirring occasionally, for 5 minutes, or until softened. Meanwhile, roughly chop half the olives. Stir the chopped and whole olives into the pan with the tomatoes and capers and

season to taste with salt and pepper. Bring to a boil, then reduce the heat, cover, and simmer gently, stirring occasionally, for 15 minutes.

2 Add the swordfish steaks to the pan and return to a boil. Cover and simmer, turning the fish once,

for 20 minutes, or until the fish is cooked and the flesh flakes easily. Transfer the fish to serving plates and spoon the sauce over them. Garnish with parsley and serve immediately.

tuna with baby vegetables

cook: 6–8 mins

prep: 5 mins, plus 1 hr marinating

serves 4

Tuna is often served in the same way as steak—that is, slightly rare in the middle. If you prefer your fish well done, then cook the tuna for an additional 1–2 minutes on each side.

NUTRITIONAL INFORMATION	
Calories	400
Protein	45g
Carbohydrate	6g
Sugars	3g
Fat	23g
Saturates	4g

INGREDIENTS

5 tbsp olive oil

2 tbsp lemon juice

1 tbsp lime juice

salt and pepper

4 tuna steaks, about 6 oz/175 g each

8 baby leeks

8 asparagus spears

8 cherry tomatoes

4 baby zucchini, halved lengthwise

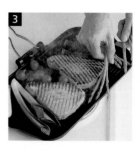

cook's tip

Depending on the size of your pan, you may need to cook this dish in 2 batches. A skillet with a ridged surface will give the tuna an attractive grilled appearance.

1 Place 4 tablespoons of the oil in a shallow, nonmetallic dish with the lemon juice and lime juice, and season to taste. Add the fish, turning to coat, then cover and let marinate in the refrigerator for 1 hour.

2 Heat a heavy-bottomed, ridged skillet and brush with the remaining oil. Drain the tuna steaks, season to taste with salt and pepper, and add to the pan. Cook over high heat for 3–4 minutes, then turn. Add the baby leeks, asparagus, cherry tomatoes, and baby zucchini. Cook for an additional 3–4 minutes, then serve.

goan fish curry

serves 4   **prep: 10 mins, plus ↺ 20 mins standing**   **cook: 15 mins ⏲**

Goan cuisine is famous for seafood and vindaloo dishes, which tend to be very hot. This recipe is a mild curry, but very flavorsome.

INGREDIENTS

1 lb 10 oz/750 g angler fish fillet, cut into chunks
1 tbsp cider vinegar
1 tsp salt
1 tsp ground turmeric
3 tbsp vegetable oil
2 garlic cloves, crushed
1 small onion, finely chopped
2 tsp ground coriander

1 tsp cayenne pepper
2 tsp paprika
2 tbsp cold water
2 tbsp tamarind pulp
2 tbsp boiling water
3 oz/85 g coconut cream, cut into pieces
1¼ cups warm water
fresh cilantro leaves, to garnish
freshly cooked rice, to serve

NUTRITIONAL INFORMATION	
Calories	.302
Protein	.31g
Carbohydrate	.8g
Sugars	.7g
Fat	.17g
Saturates	.7g

variation

You could use any firm white fish to make this curry. Try substituting chunks of cod for the angler fish.

cook's tip

Tamarind pulp is made from the pressed pods of the tamarind tree. If you are unable to find it, substitute lemon or lime juice for the tamarind juice made in Step 3.

1 Place the fish on a plate and drizzle over the vinegar. Mix half the salt and half the turmeric together and sprinkle evenly over the angler fish. Cover and let stand for 20 minutes.

2 Heat the oil in a large, heavy-bottomed skillet and add the garlic. Brown slightly, then add the onion and cook over low heat, stirring occasionally, for 3–4 minutes, or until soft but not browned. Add the ground cilantro and stir for 1 minute.

3 Place the remaining turmeric and salt in a bowl with the cayenne pepper, paprika, and cold water and stir to make a paste. Add to the skillet and cook for 1–2 minutes. Stir the tamarind pulp and boiling water together in a bowl. When thickened and the pulp has come away from the seeds, push through a strainer with the back of a wooden spoon. Discard the seeds.

4 Add the coconut cream, warm water, and tamarind paste to the skillet and stir until the coconut has dissolved. Add the fish and any juices on the plate and simmer gently for 4–5 minutes, or until the sauce has thickened and the fish is just tender. Serve on a bed of freshly cooked rice, garnished with fresh cilantro.

spanish fish in tomato sauce

cook: 45 mins

**prep: 15 mins,
plus 1 hr marinating**

serves 4

This robust and colorful Spanish sauce would go well with most white fish and you can use either fillets or steaks.

INGREDIENTS

4 tbsp lemon juice

6 tbsp olive oil

salt and pepper

4 swordfish steaks,
about 6 oz/175 g each

1 onion, finely chopped

1 garlic clove, finely chopped

1 tbsp all-purpose flour

8 oz/225 g tomatoes, peeled,
seeded, and chopped

1 tbsp tomato paste

1¼ cups dry white wine

fresh dill sprigs, to garnish

variation

Thick cod steaks will take on the flavor of this tomato sauce just as well as the swordfish, if you prefer.

cook's tip

When choosing fresh fish steaks, look for firm flesh and a fresh smell. Store the fish in the refrigerator and use it within 24 hours.

1 Preheat the oven to 350°F/180°C. Place the lemon juice and 4 tablespoons of the olive oil in a shallow, nonmetallic dish, stir well, then season to taste with salt and pepper. Add the swordfish steaks, turning to coat thoroughly, then cover with plastic wrap and let marinate in the refrigerator for 1 hour.

2 Heat the remaining oil in a flameproof casserole. Add the onion and cook over low heat, stirring occasionally, for 10 minutes, or until golden. Add the garlic and cook, stirring frequently, for 2 minutes. Sprinkle in the flour and cook, stirring, for 1 minute, then add the tomatoes, tomato paste, and wine. Bring to a boil, stirring.

3 Add the fish to the casserole, pushing it down into the liquid. Cover and cook in the preheated oven for 20 minutes, or until cooked through and the flesh flakes easily. Serve garnished with dill sprigs.

paella del mar

serves 6   prep: 45 mins   cook: 25–30 mins

Paella is actually the name of the pan in which this famous Spanish dish is cooked—a large, heavy-bottomed skillet or casserole is a good substitute. This fish and shellfish version comes from Valencia.

INGREDIENTS

1 lb/450 g live mussels

6 squid

½ cup olive oil

1 Spanish onion, chopped

2 garlic cloves, finely chopped

1 red bell pepper, seeded and cut into strips

1 green bell pepper, seeded and cut into strips

14 oz/400 g risotto rice

2 tomatoes, peeled and chopped

1 tbsp tomato paste

6 oz/175 g angler fish fillet, cut into chunks

6 oz/175 g red snapper fillet, cut into chunks

6 oz/175 g cod fillet, cut into chunks

generous 2 cups Fish Stock (see page 13)

4 oz/115 g fresh or frozen green beans, halved

4 oz/115 g fresh or frozen peas

6 canned artichoke hearts, drained

¼ tsp saffron threads

salt and pepper

12 raw jumbo shrimp

NUTRITIONAL INFORMATION

Calories	.623
Protein	.48g
Carbohydrate	.68g
Sugars	.7g
Fat	.19g
Saturates	.2g

variation

Any kind of firm-fleshed fish can be used in this paella. You could also experiment with other vegetables, such as chopped zucchini or asparagus.

cook's tip

Authentic paella is made with round grain Valencia rice, but this is difficult to obtain outside Spain. Risotto rice is a good substitute, or you could use long-grain rice, although this will tend to stick to the pan.

1 Clean the mussels by scrubbing or scraping the shells and pulling off any beards. Discard any with broken shells or any that refuse to close when tapped with a knife. Rinse the mussels under cold running water.

2 To prepare each squid, pull the pouch and tentacles apart, then remove the innards from the pouch. Slice the tentacles away from the head and discard the head. Rinse the pouch and tentacles under cold running water.

3 Heat the oil in a paella pan or flameproof casserole. Add the onion, garlic, and bell peppers. Cook over medium heat, stirring, for 5 minutes, or until softened.

Add the squid and cook for 2 minutes. Add the rice and cook, stirring, until transparent and coated with oil.

4 Add the tomatoes, tomato paste, and fish and cook for 3 minutes, then add the Stock. Gently stir in the beans, peas, artichoke hearts, and saffron and season to taste with salt and pepper.

5 Arrange the mussels around the edge of the pan and top the mixture with the shrimp. Bring to a boil, reduce the heat, and simmer, shaking the pan from time to time, for 15–20 minutes, or until the rice is tender. Discard any mussels that remain closed. Serve straight from the pan.

jansson's temptation

cook: 1 hr   **prep: 10 mins**   **serves 4**

NUTRITIONAL INFORMATION

Calories	373
Protein	8g
Carbohydrate	29g
Sugars	8g
Fat	26g
Saturates	15g

variation

If fresh parsley is unavailable, then use 2–3 teaspoons of dried or freeze-dried parsley instead.

Jansson was a Swedish opera singer, as famous for his liaisons as his singing. Favored guests visited his rooms after a performance, where he cooked for them. This was one of the meals they enjoyed.

INGREDIENTS

3 tbsp butter, plus extra for greasing
14 anchovy fillets
1 lb/450 g potatoes, grated
2 onions, sliced

1 garlic clove, finely chopped
1 tbsp chopped fresh parsley
pepper
1¼ cups light cream
fresh parsley sprigs, to garnish

cook's tip

If you use canned anchovy fillets, you can drizzle a little of the oil over the potatoes before adding the cream in Step 2. If using salted anchovy fillets, soak them in water or milk before filleting them.

1 Preheat the oven to 400°F/200°C. Generously grease an ovenproof dish with butter. Cut each anchovy fillet into 4 pieces.

2 Layer the grated potatoes, onion slices, garlic, parsley, and anchovies in the dish, ending with a layer of potatoes, seasoning each layer with pepper. Pour half the cream over the top and dot with the butter.

3 Bake in the preheated oven for 35–40 minutes, or until the potatoes are just colored, then pour over the remaining cream and bake for an additional 20–25 minutes, or until the topping is golden and tender. Serve immediately, garnished with fresh parsley sprigs.

angler fish with onions & cilantro

cook: 20 mins

prep: 15 mins, plus 1 hr marinating

serves 4

NUTRITIONAL INFORMATION	
Calories	265
Protein	45g
Carbohydrate	6g
Sugars	4g
Fat	7g
Saturates	1g

variation

Substitute green chiles for the red chiles if you would prefer a slightly more bitter spiciness in this dish.

Angler fish is popular not just because of its fine flavor and firm texture, but also because there are none of the little bones that sometimes put people off fish. It is a meaty fish, so all you need to accompany it is a helping of salad greens.

INGREDIENTS

2 lb 4 oz/1 kg angler fish tail	1 Spanish onion, sliced into rings
4 tbsp lime juice	2 fresh red chiles, seeded and
1 garlic clove, finely chopped	finely chopped
1 tsp ground cumin	1 tbsp chopped fresh cilantro
1 tsp paprika	2 tbsp olive oil
salt and pepper	fresh cilantro leaves, to garnish

cook's tip

Be careful not to let the angler fish fillets marinate for more than 1 hour, otherwise the lime juice will begin to "cook" the flesh.

1 Preheat the oven to 425°F/220°C. Remove the grey membrane that covers the angler fish tail with a sharp knife, then cut along one side of the central bone to remove the fillet of flesh. Repeat the process on the other side to remove the other fillet from the bone, then tie the 2 fillets together with kitchen string. Transfer the tied fillets to a shallow, nonmetallic, ovenproof dish.

2 Place the lime juice, garlic, cumin, and paprika in a bowl, stir to mix, and season to taste with salt and pepper. Spoon the marinade over the angler fish, cover, and let marinate in the refrigerator for 1 hour.

3 Sprinkle the onion rings, chiles, and chopped cilantro over the fish and drizzle with the oil. Roast in the preheated oven for 20 minutes, or until cooked through and the flesh flakes easily. Cut the fish into slices, garnish with fresh cilantro leaves, and serve.

cotriade

serves 4   **prep: 15 mins, plus 🕐 10 mins standing**   **cook: 45 mins 🕐**

This is a rich French stew of fish and vegetables, flavored with saffron and fresh herbs. To serve it traditionally, ladle it over the slices of thick crusty bread, rather than serving it separately.

INGREDIENTS

large pinch of saffron threads	2 bay leaves
2½ cups hot Fish Stock	4 ripe tomatoes, peeled and chopped
(see page 13)	2 lb/900 g mixed fish fillets,
1 tbsp olive oil	such as haddock, hake, and mackerel,
2 tbsp butter	coarsely chopped
1 onion, sliced	2 tbsp chopped fresh parsley
2 garlic cloves, chopped	salt and pepper
1 lb/450 g potatoes, cut into chunks	crusty bread, to serve
1 leek, sliced	
1 small fennel bulb, thinly sliced	TO GARNISH
⅔ cup dry white wine	lemon slices
1 tbsp fresh thyme leaves	fresh dill sprigs

NUTRITIONAL INFORMATION

Calories	81
Protein	. . . . .7.4g
Carbohydrate	. . . . .4g
Sugars	. . . . .1g
Fat	. . . . .4g
Saturates	. . . . .1g

variation

Use as wide a variety of fish as possible to make this soup—such as chunks of red snapper, pompano, sea bass, cod, sole, or tilapia, or even eels.

cook's tip

Once the fish and vegetables have been cooked, you could process the soup in a blender or food processor and strain it to give a smooth fish soup.

1 Place the saffron in a mortar and crush with a pestle, then add it to the Fish Stock. Stir the mixture and let stand for at least 10 minutes.

2 Heat the olive oil and butter in a large, heavy-bottomed pan or flameproof casserole. Add the onion and cook over low heat, stirring occasionally, for 4–5 minutes, or until softened. Add the garlic, potatoes, leek, and fennel. Cover and cook for an additional 10–15 minutes, until the vegetables are softened.

3 Add the white wine and simmer rapidly for 3–4 minutes, or until reduced by about half. Add the thyme, bay leaves, and tomatoes and stir well. Add the saffron-infused Fish Stock. Bring to a boil, reduce the heat to low, cover, and simmer for 15 minutes, or until the vegetables are tender.

4 Add the fish, return to a boil, and simmer for an additional 3–4 minutes, or until the fish is tender. Add the parsley and season to taste with salt and pepper. Transfer the fish and vegetables to separate warmed serving dishes with a perforated spoon and garnish with lemon slices and fresh dill sprigs. Serve with crusty bread.

moroccan fish tagine

cook: 1 hr 15 mins   **prep: 10 mins**   **serves 4**

variation

You can use chopped fresh tomatoes instead of canned tomatoes if you wish, but add 1 tablespoon of tomato paste in Step 2 to give extra flavor.

A tagine is a Moroccan cooking vessel consisting of an earthenware dish with a domed lid that has a steam hole in the top.

INGREDIENTS

2 tbsp olive oil

1 large onion, finely chopped

pinch of saffron threads

½ tsp ground cinnamon

1 tsp ground coriander

½ tsp ground cumin

½ tsp ground turmeric

7 oz/200 g canned chopped tomatoes

1¼ cups Fish Stock (see page 13)

4 small red snappers, cleaned, boned, and heads and tails removed

2 oz/55 g pitted green olives

1 tbsp chopped preserved lemon

3 tbsp chopped fresh cilantro

salt and pepper

freshly cooked couscous, to serve

cook's tip

To preserve lemons, cut them into fourths lengthwise without cutting right through, then pack in a jar with 2 oz/55 g of sea salt per lemon. Add the juice of 1 lemon, cover with water, and store for 1 month.

1 Heat the olive oil in a flameproof casserole. Add the onion and cook gently over very low heat, stirring occasionally, for 10 minutes, or until softened, but not colored. Add the saffron, cinnamon, ground coriander, cumin, and turmeric and cook for an additional 30 seconds, stirring constantly.

2 Add the tomatoes and Fish Stock and stir well. Bring to a boil, reduce the heat, cover, and simmer for 15 minutes. Uncover and simmer for 20–35 minutes, or until thickened.

3 Cut each red snapper in half, then add the fish pieces to the casserole, pushing them down into the liquid. Simmer the stew for an additional 5–6 minutes, or until the fish is just cooked.

4 Carefully stir in the olives, lemon, and fresh cilantro. Season to taste with salt and pepper and serve immediately with couscous.

mussels cooked with lager

serves 4 | **prep: 25 mins** | **cook: 15 mins**

Mussels cooked in beer, tomatoes, and hot Mexican spices make a sophisticated and attractive dish for a summertime dinner party, and are sure to be a talking point for your guests.

INGREDIENTS

3 lb 5 oz/1.5 kg live mussels

2 cups lager

2 onions, chopped

5 garlic cloves, coarsely chopped

1 fresh green chile, such as jalapeño or serrano, seeded and thinly sliced

6 oz/175 g fresh tomatoes, diced, or canned chopped tomatoes

2–3 tbsp chopped fresh cilantro

NUTRITIONAL INFORMATION	
Calories 163	
Protein 21g	
Carbohydrate 7g	
Sugars 6g	
Fat 3g	
Saturates 1g	

cook's tip

Add the kernels of 2 corn cobs to the lager mixture in Step 2. A pinch of sugar might be required to bring out the sweetness of the corn.

1 Clean the mussels by scrubbing or scraping the shells and pulling off any beards that are attached to them. Discard any with broken shells or any that refuse to close when tapped with a knife. Rinse the mussels under cold running water.

2 Place the lager, onions, garlic, chile slices, and tomatoes in a large, heavy-bottomed pan. Bring to a boil. Add the mussels, then cover and cook over medium heat for 10 minutes, or until the shells open. Discard any that remain closed.

3 Ladle into individual bowls and serve sprinkled with fresh cilantro.

moules marinières

⏱ **cook: 10 mins**   🕐 **prep: 25 mins**   **serves 4**

Served with plenty of fresh crusty French bread, this is a shellfish-lover's feast. The only extra treat you need to make this into a perfect meal is a glass of chilled white wine.

NUTRITIONAL INFORMATION	
Calories	185
Protein	26g
Carbohydrate	2g
Sugars	1g
Fat	3g
Saturates	1g

INGREDIENTS

4 lb 8 oz/2 kg live mussels

1¼ cups dry white wine

6 shallots, finely chopped

1 bouquet garni

pepper

crusty bread, to serve

cook's tip

Never eat mussels that you have collected from the beach yourself, as they may have been polluted and could cause serious illness.

1 Clean the mussels by scrubbing or scraping the shells and pulling off any beards. Discard any with broken shells or any that refuse to close when tapped with a knife. Rinse the mussels under cold running water.

2 Pour the wine into a large, heavy-bottomed pan, add the shallots and bouquet garni, and season to taste with pepper. Bring to a boil over medium heat. Add the mussels, cover tightly, and cook, shaking the pan occasionally, for 5 minutes. Remove and discard the bouquet garni and any mussels that remain closed.

3 Divide the mussels between 4 soup plates with a perforated spoon. Tilt the casserole to let any sand settle, then spoon the cooking liquid over the mussels and serve immediately with bread.

provençal-style mussels

serves 4   **prep: 10 mins** ⟳   **cook: 50 mins** ⟳

These delicious large mussels are served hot with a flavorsome tomato and vegetable sauce. Mop up the mouthwatering sauce with a helping of some fresh crusty bread.

INGREDIENTS

1 tbsp olive oil	2 tbsp tomato paste
1 large onion, finely chopped	1 tsp superfine sugar
1 garlic clove, finely chopped	1¾ oz/50 g pitted black olives in brine,
1 small red bell pepper, seeded and	drained and chopped
finely chopped	1 lb 8 oz/675 g cooked New Zealand
1 fresh rosemary sprig	mussels in their shells
2 bay leaves	1 tsp grated orange rind
14 oz/400 g canned chopped tomatoes	2 tbsp chopped fresh parsley,
⅔ cup white wine	to garnish
salt and pepper	crusty bread, to serve
1 zucchini, finely diced	

NUTRITIONAL INFORMATION

Calories	.253
Protein	.31g
Carbohydrate	.9g
Sugars	.8g
Fat	.8g
Saturates	.1g

variation

You can substitute a fresh thyme sprig for the rosemary, if you prefer, or use it in addition to the rosemary.

cook's tip

Check that none of the cooked mussels have damaged shells—discard any that are broken before steaming the remainder in Step 3.

1 Heat the olive oil in a large pan and cook the onion, garlic, and bell pepper over low heat for 3–4 minutes, or until softened.

2 Add the rosemary sprig and bay leaves to the pan, then add the tomatoes and a scant ½ cup of the wine. Season to taste with salt and pepper. Bring to a boil, reduce the heat, and simmer for 15 minutes. Stir in the zucchini, tomato paste, sugar, and olives and simmer for an additional 10 minutes.

3 Meanwhile, bring a large pan of water to a boil. Arrange the cooked mussels in a steamer and place over the pan. Sprinkle with the remaining wine and orange rind. Cover and steam until the mussels open. Discard any that remain closed.

4 Remove the mussels with a perforated spoon and arrange on a serving plate. Discard the herbs and spoon the sauce over the mussels. Garnish with parsley and serve with crusty bread.

thai shrimp curry

cook: 10 mins   **prep: 15 mins**   **serves 4**

NUTRITIONAL INFORMATION

Calories 150

Protein 11g

Carbohydrate 6g

Sugars 4g

Fat 9g

Saturates 1g

Thai cooking is renowned for its subtle blending of aromatic spices, and this mouthwatering curry is no exception.

INGREDIENTS

1 lb/450 g raw jumbo shrimp

2 tbsp peanut oil

2 tbsp Thai green curry paste

4 kaffir lime leaves, shredded

1 lemon grass stem, chopped

scant 1 cup coconut milk

2 tbsp Thai fish sauce

½ cucumber, seeded and cut into thin sticks

12 fresh basil leaves, plus extra to garnish

2 fresh green chiles, sliced

variation

Replace the fresh basil leaves with the same amount of fresh cilantro leaves. If you prefer a milder curry, seed the fresh chiles before slicing.

cook's tip

Three types of basil are used in Thailand: hairy (*bai mangluk*), sweet (*bai horapa*), and Thai or holy basil (*bai grapao*). They are all more strongly flavored than Western basil.

1 Peel and devein the shrimp. Heat the peanut oil in a preheated wok or heavy-bottomed skillet. Add the curry paste and cook over medium heat for 1 minute, or until it is bubbling and releases its aroma. Add the shrimp, lime leaves, and lemon grass and stir-fry for 2 minutes, or until the shrimp have turned pink.

2 Stir in the coconut milk and bring to a boil, then reduce the heat and simmer, stirring occasionally, for 5 minutes. Stir in the fish sauce, cucumber, and basil. Transfer to a warmed serving dish. Scatter over the chile slices, garnish with fresh basil leaves, and serve.

sweet & sour shrimp

serves 4   **prep: 10 mins** ⟲   **cook: 5 mins** ⟳

The rich flavors of dark soy sauce and sesame oil are perfectly complemented by the tangy fresh gingerroot and rich brown sugar in this Eastern stir-fry.

INGREDIENTS

4 scallions, finely chopped, plus extra to garnish

2 tsp finely chopped fresh gingerroot

1 lb/450 g cooked jumbo shrimp

1 tbsp peanut or corn oil

2 tbsp dark soy sauce

2 tbsp brown sugar

3 tbsp rice vinegar

1 tbsp Chinese rice wine

½ cup Fish or Chicken Stock (see page 13)

1 tsp cornstarch

1–2 tbsp water

dash of sesame oil

shredded Napa cabbage, to serve

NUTRITIONAL INFORMATION	
Calories 143	
Protein 10g	
Carbohydrate 16g	
Sugars 8g	
Fat 4g	
Saturates 1g	

variation

To serve with noodles, break up 8 oz/ 225 g of rice vermicelli into short lengths, heat 4 tablespoons of oil in the wok, and stir-fry in batches.

cook's tip

Rather than discarding shrimp heads and shells, you can use them to make a delicately flavored shellfish stock by simmering them gently in enough water to cover.

1 Finely chop the scallions, and peel and finely chop the fresh gingerroot. Peel and devein the shrimp, pat dry with paper towels and reserve.

2 Heat the oil in a preheated wok or large skillet. Add the scallions and gingerroot and stir-fry over high heat for 1 minute. Add the soy sauce, sugar, vinegar, rice wine, and Stock and bring to a boil.

3 Place the cornstarch and water in a small bowl and mix to make a paste. Stir 1 tablespoon of the paste into the sauce and add the shrimp. Cook, stirring, until slightly thickened and smooth. Sprinkle with sesame oil.

4 Make a bed of Napa cabbage leaves on 4 serving plates and top with shrimp and sauce. Garnish with shredded scallion tassels and serve immediately.

spicy squid

⏱ **cook: 5–10 mins**   ⏱ **prep: 15 mins**   **serves 4**

NUTRITIONAL INFORMATION

Calories	137
Protein	18g
Carbohydrate	1g
Sugars	0g
Fat	7g
Saturates	1g

variation

Chop 3½–5 oz/100–140 g of thawed peeled shrimp, add 1 tablespoon of chopped dill and 2 chopped shallots, then use to fill the squid pouches.

This recipe works best with delicate baby squid, but if you can obtain only larger squid, slice the bodies into thick rings and cut the tentacles in half before you begin cooking.

INGREDIENTS

1 lb/450 g baby squid

2 tbsp olive oil

1 bunch of fresh parsley, finely chopped

4 garlic cloves, crushed

1 tbsp grated lemon rind

1 tbsp lemon juice

salt and pepper

fresh flatleaf parsley sprigs, to garnish

cook's tip

If you don't want to use a pan for this dish, you can also cook the squid under a preheated hot broiler or on a lit barbecue grill, turning frequently and brushing with olive oil.

1 To prepare each squid, pull the pouch and tentacles apart, then remove the remaining innards from the pouch. Slice the tentacles away from the head and discard the head. Rinse the pouch and tentacles under cold running water.

2 Heat a heavy-bottomed ridged skillet and brush with oil. Add the squid pouches and tentacles and cook over medium heat, turning and brushing with more oil occasionally, for 5–10 minutes, or until golden brown. Divide between 4 serving plates.

3 Place the parsley, garlic, and lemon rind in a small bowl and stir to mix. Sprinkle the lemon juice over the squid and season to taste with salt and pepper. Sprinkle the parsley mixture over the squid, garnish with parsley sprigs, and serve warm.

shellfish chili

cook: 45 mins

prep: 30 mins, plus 1 hr marinating

serves 4

variation

If you don't have time to make the Fish Stock for this dish, you can substitute the same amount of water.

For an authentic Mexican treat, serve this seafood extravaganza with ready-made tortillas, heated through in a dry skillet.

INGREDIENTS

4 oz/115 g raw shrimp, peeled

9 oz/250 g prepared scallops, thawed if frozen

4 oz/115 g angler fish fillet, cut into chunks

1 lime, peeled and thinly sliced

1 tbsp chili powder

1 tsp ground cumin

3 tbsp chopped fresh cilantro

2 garlic cloves, finely chopped

1 fresh green chile, seeded and chopped

3 tbsp corn oil

1 onion, coarsely chopped

1 red bell pepper, seeded and coarsely chopped

1 yellow bell pepper, seeded and coarsely chopped

¼ tsp ground cloves

pinch of ground cinnamon

pinch of cayenne pepper

salt

1½ cups Fish Stock (see page 13)

14 oz/400 g canned chopped tomatoes

14 oz/400 g canned red kidney beans, drained and rinsed

cook's tip

If you use any frozen seafood for this chili, make sure that it is thoroughly thawed through before you begin cooking. For a slightly milder chili, reduce the amount of chili powder added in Step 2.

1 Place the shrimp, scallops, angler fish chunks, and lime slices in a large, nonmetallic dish with ¼ teaspoon of the chili powder, ¼ teaspoon of the ground cumin, 1 tablespoon of the chopped cilantro, half the garlic, the fresh chile, and 1 tablespoon of the oil. Cover with plastic wrap and let marinate for up to 1 hour.

2 Meanwhile, heat 1 tablespoon of the remaining oil in a flameproof casserole or large, heavy-bottomed pan. Add the onion, the remaining garlic, and the red and yellow bell peppers and cook over low heat, stirring occasionally, for 5 minutes, or until softened. Add the remaining chili powder, the remaining cumin, the cloves, cinnamon, and cayenne with the remaining oil, if necessary, and season to taste with salt. Cook, stirring, for 5 minutes, then gradually stir in the Stock and the tomatoes and their juices. Partially cover and simmer for 25 minutes.

3 Add the beans to the tomato mixture and spoon the fish and shellfish on top. Cover and cook for 10 minutes, or until the fish and shellfish are cooked through. Sprinkle with the remaining cilantro and serve.

vegetarian

Nutritionists tell us that we should eat more vegetables, but it isn't always easy to persuade the family to eat up their greens, especially if they are sitting in an unappetizing heap on the side of the plate. This chapter provides the answer, with a spectacular collection of mouthwatering vegetable dishes, from Mediterranean-style Greek Beans (see page 156) to a delicious and unusual Winter Vegetable Cobbler (see page 167).

Beans, lentils, bell peppers, zucchini, eggplants, broccoli, cauliflower, onions, tomatoes, and even the humble potato take a starring role, and are combined with each other for a colorful, melt-in-the-mouth medley which will satisfy even the hungriest appetite. If you are in the mood for something hot, try Vegetable Chili (see page 161), Yellow Curry (see page 164), or Spiced Cashew Nut Curry (see page 165). If you are looking for something a little more comforting, Cauliflower Bake (see page 168) or Bell Pepper & Mushroom Hash (see page 157) will fit the bill perfectly.

A vegetarian main course is an easy way to ring the changes in the weekly menu, and nut- or pulse-based dishes can be just as nutritious as a meat or fish dish. Whatever your favorite vegetable, there will be something in this section to tempt even the most reluctant meat-eater to try something a little different.

greek beans

serves 4   **prep: 5 mins**   **cook: 1 hr 5 mins**

This dish contains many typical Greek flavors, such as lemon and garlic, for a really flavorsome recipe. The fresh oregano and black olives give it a real taste of the Mediterranean.

INGREDIENTS

14 oz/400 g canned haricot
beans, drained

1 tbsp olive oil

3 garlic cloves, crushed

generous 1¾ cups Vegetable Stock
(see page 13)

1 bay leaf

2 fresh oregano sprigs

1 tbsp tomato paste

juice of 1 lemon

1 small red onion, chopped

1 oz/25 g pitted black olives, halved

salt and pepper

NUTRITIONAL INFORMATION

Calories 115

Protein 6g

Carbohydrate 15g

Sugars 4g

Fat 4g

Saturates 0.6g

cook's tip

You can substitute other canned beans for the Great Northern beans—try cannellini beans, black-eye peas, or chickpeas. Drain and rinse before use—canned beans often have sugar or salt added.

1 Put the Great Northern beans into a flameproof casserole dish, add the oil and crushed garlic, and cook over low heat, stirring occasionally, for 4–5 minutes.

2 Add the Stock, bay leaf, oregano, tomato paste, lemon juice, and red onion and stir to mix. Cover and simmer for 1 hour, or until the sauce has thickened.

3 Stir in the black olives, then season the beans to taste with salt and pepper. The dish is delicious served either warm or cold.

bell pepper & mushroom hash

⏲ **cook: 30 mins**　　　　⏱ **prep: 10 mins**　　　　**serves 4**

This quick and easy-to-prepare one-pan dish is ideal for an evening snack. Packed with color and flavor, it is an extremely versatile recipe—you can add whichever vegetables you have to hand.

NUTRITIONAL INFORMATION

Calories 182

Protein 5g

Carbohydrate 34g

Sugars 6g

Fat 4g

Saturates 0.5g

INGREDIENTS

1 lb 8 oz/675 g potatoes, cut into cubes

salt and pepper

1 tbsp olive oil

2 garlic cloves, crushed

1 green bell pepper, seeded
and cut into cubes

1 yellow bell pepper, seeded
and cut into cubes

3 tomatoes, diced

2¾ oz/75 g white mushrooms, halved

1 tbsp Worcestershire sauce

2 tbsp chopped fresh basil

fresh basil sprigs, to garnish

warm crusty bread, to serve

cook's tip

Most brands of Worcestershire sauce contain anchovies, so if you are a vegetarian, check the label to make sure you choose a vegetarian variety.

1 Cook the potato cubes in a pan of lightly salted boiling water for 7–8 minutes. Drain well and reserve.

2 Heat the olive oil in a large, heavy-bottomed skillet. Add the potato cubes and cook over medium heat, stirring, for 8–10 minutes, until browned.

3 Add the crushed garlic and bell pepper cubes and cook, stirring frequently, for 2–3 minutes.

4 Add the tomatoes and mushrooms and cook, stirring frequently, for 5–6 minutes, then stir in the Worcestershire sauce and basil and season to taste.

5 Transfer to a warmed serving dish, garnish with basil leaves, and serve with warm crusty bread.

sweet & sour vegetables

serves 4   **prep: 15 mins, plus
30 mins standing**   **cook: 30 mins**

*This is a dish of Persian origin—not Chinese, as it sounds. Plump
diced eggplants are cooked and mixed with tomatoes, mint, sugar,
and vinegar to give a unique combination of flavors.*

INGREDIENTS

2 large eggplants	3 tbsp chopped fresh mint
salt and pepper	⅔ cup Vegetable Stock
6 tbsp olive oil	(see page 13)
4 garlic cloves, crushed	4 tsp brown sugar
1 onion, cut into eighths	2 tbsp red wine vinegar
4 large tomatoes, seeded	1 tsp chili flakes
and chopped	fresh mint sprigs, to garnish

NUTRITIONAL INFORMATION

Calories	.218
Protein	.3g
Carbohydrate	.14g
Sugars	.12g
Fat	.17g
Saturates	.3g

variation

Substitute 1 teaspoon of chopped
fresh red chile for the chili flakes to
give the dish a slightly milder flavor.

cook's tip

Choose firm, glossy eggplants
for this dish. Large eggplants
benefit from salting to extract
their juices—small eggplants
are less bitter, and can often
be cooked without salting.

1 Cut the eggplants
into cubes. Place them
in a colander, sprinkle with
plenty of salt, and let stand for
30 minutes to remove all the
bitter juices. Rinse thoroughly
under cold running water and
pat dry with paper towels.

2 Heat the oil in a large,
heavy-bottomed skillet.
Add the eggplant and cook
over medium heat, stirring,
for 1–2 minutes, or until
beginning to color. Stir in the
garlic and onion wedges and
cook, stirring constantly, for
an additional 2–3 minutes.

3 Stir in the tomatoes,
mint and Stock. Reduce
the heat, cover, and simmer for
15–20 minutes, or until the
eggplant is tender.

4 Add the brown sugar,
red wine vinegar, and
chili flakes, then season to
taste with salt and pepper
and cook for an additional
2–3 minutes, stirring.

5 Transfer to a warmed
serving dish, garnish
with fresh mint sprigs, and
serve immediately.

vegetable chili

cook: 1 hr 20 mins   **prep: 10 mins**   **serves 4**

NUTRITIONAL INFORMATION

Calories 213

Protein 12g

Carbohydrate 21g

Sugars 11g

Fat 10g

Saturates 5g

variation

If you prefer a hotter dish, stir in a little extra chili powder when you adjust the seasoning at the end of Step 4.

This is a hearty and flavorsome dish that works well served on its own, and is delicious spooned over cooked rice or baked potatoes to make a more substantial meal.

INGREDIENTS

1 eggplant, cut into 1-inch/2.5-cm slices

1 tbsp olive oil, plus extra for brushing

1 large red or yellow onion, finely chopped

2 red or yellow bell peppers, seeded and finely chopped

3–4 garlic cloves, finely chopped or crushed

1 lb 12 oz/800 g canned chopped tomatoes

1 tbsp mild chili powder

½ tsp ground cumin

½ tsp dried oregano

salt and pepper

2 small zucchini, cut into fourths lengthwise and sliced

14 oz/400 g canned kidney beans, drained and rinsed

scant 2 cups water

1 tbsp tomato paste

6 scallions, finely chopped

scant 1¼ cups grated Cheddar cheese

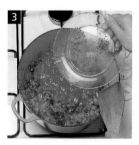

cook's tip

If you would prefer to leave the purple eggplant skin out of this chili, you can peel the eggplant before cutting it into slices.

1 Brush the eggplant slices on one side with oil. Heat half the oil in a large, heavy-bottomed skillet. Add the eggplant slices, oiled-side up, and cook over medium heat for 5–6 minutes, or until browned on one side. Turn the slices over, cook on the other side until browned, and transfer to a plate. Cut into bite-size pieces.

2 Heat the remaining oil in a large pan over medium heat. Add the chopped onion and bell peppers to the pan and cook, stirring occasionally, for 3–4 minutes, or until the onion is just softened, but not browned. Add the garlic and cook for an additional 2–3 minutes, or until the onion just begins to color.

3 Add the tomatoes, chili powder, cumin, and oregano. Season to taste with salt and pepper. Bring just to a boil, reduce the heat, cover, and simmer gently for 15 minutes.

4 Add the zucchini, eggplant, and kidney beans. Stir in the water and tomato paste. Return to a boil, then cover the pan and simmer for an additional 45 minutes, or until the vegetables are tender. Taste and adjust the seasoning, if necessary.

5 Ladle into warmed bowls and top with chopped scallions and cheese.

vegetable curry

serves 4 **prep: 10 mins** ⟳ **cook: 45 mins** ⟳

*This colorful and interesting mixture of vegetables, cooked in
a spicy sauce, is excellent served with rice and naan bread.*

INGREDIENTS

1 eggplant	2 tsp ground coriander
8 oz/225 g turnips	1 tbsp mild or medium curry powder
12 oz/350 g new potatoes	scant 2 cups Vegetable Stock
8 oz/225 g cauliflower	(see page 13)
8 oz/225 g white mushrooms	14 oz/400 g canned chopped tomatoes
1 large onion	salt
3 carrots	1 green bell pepper, seeded and sliced
6 tbsp ghee	1 tbsp cornstarch
2 garlic cloves, crushed	⅔ cup coconut milk
4 tsp finely chopped fresh gingerroot	2–3 tbsp ground almonds
1–2 fresh green chiles, seeded	fresh cilantro sprigs, to garnish
and chopped	freshly cooked rice, to serve
1 tbsp paprika	

NUTRITIONAL INFORMATION

Calories	.421
Protein	.12g
Carbohydrate	.42g
Sugars	.20g
Fat	.24g
Saturates	.3g

variation

You can use vegetable oil instead
of the ghee, and substitute peeled
rutabaga for the turnip, if you prefer.

cook's tip

Ghee is clarified butter,
which contains no milk solids.
It can be heated to much
higher temperatures than
ordinary butter. It is available
from Indian specialist stores
and major food stores.

1 Cut the eggplant,
turnips, and potatoes
into ½-inch/1-cm cubes. Divide
the cauliflower into small
florets. The white mushrooms
can be used whole or sliced
thickly, if preferred. Slice the
onion and carrots.

2 Heat the ghee in a
large pan. Add the
onion, turnip, potato, and
cauliflower and cook over low
heat, stirring frequently, for
3 minutes. Add the garlic,
gingerroot, chiles, paprika,
ground coriander, and curry
powder and cook, stirring,
for 1 minute.

3 Add the Stock,
tomatoes, eggplant,
and mushrooms and season
with salt. Cover and simmer,
stirring occasionally, for
30 minutes, or until tender.
Add the green bell pepper
and carrots, cover, and cook
for an additional 5 minutes.

4 Place the cornstarch
and coconut milk in a
bowl, mix into a smooth paste,
and stir into the vegetable
mixture. Add the ground
almonds and simmer, stirring

constantly, for 2 minutes. Taste
and adjust the seasoning, if
necessary. Transfer to serving
plates, garnish with cilantro
sprigs, and serve immediately
with freshly cooked rice.

yellow curry

serves 4   prep: 10 mins   cook: 15 mins

Potatoes are not highly regarded in Thai cooking because rice is the traditional staple food, but this dish is a tasty exception.

INGREDIENTS

2 garlic cloves, finely chopped

1¼-inch/3-cm piece of galangal, finely chopped

1 lemon grass stem, finely chopped

1 tsp coriander seeds

3 tbsp vegetable oil

2 tsp Thai red curry paste

½ tsp ground turmeric

generous ¾ cup coconut milk

9 oz/250 g potatoes, cut into cubes

scant ½ cup Vegetable Stock (see page 13)

7 oz/200 g fresh young spinach leaves

1 small onion, thinly sliced into rings

NUTRITIONAL INFORMATION	
Calories 160	
Protein 3g	
Carbohydrate 15g	
Sugars 4g	
Fat 10g	
Saturates 1g	

cook's tip

Choose a firm, waxy potato for this dish, one that will keep its shape during cooking, in preference to a floury variety that will break up easily.

1 Put the garlic, galangal, lemon grass, and coriander seeds into a mortar and crush with a pestle to make a smooth paste.

2 Heat 2 tablespoons of the oil in a large, heavy-bottomed skillet or preheated wok. Stir in the fresh garlic and spice paste and stir-fry over high heat for 30 seconds, then stir in the curry paste and turmeric, add the coconut milk, and bring to a boil.

3 Add the potatoes and Stock. Return to a boil, then reduce the heat and simmer, uncovered, for 10–12 minutes, or until the potatoes are almost tender. Stir in the spinach and simmer until the leaves have wilted.

4 Heat the remaining oil in a separate skillet, add the onion, and cook until crisp and golden brown. Place on top of the curry just before serving.

spiced cashew nut curry

cook: 25 mins　　　　**prep: 15 mins, plus 8 hrs soaking**　　　　**serves 4**

This unusual vegetarian dish is best served as a side dish with other curries and with rice to soak up the wonderfully rich, spiced juices.

NUTRITIONAL INFORMATION

Calories 455

Protein 13g

Carbohydrate 16g

Sugars 6g

Fat 39g

Saturates 11g

INGREDIENTS

9 oz/250 g unsalted cashew nuts

1 small fresh green chile

1 tsp coriander seeds

1 tsp cumin seeds

2 cardamom pods, crushed

1 tbsp corn oil

1 onion, thinly sliced

1 garlic clove, crushed

1 cinnamon stick

½ tsp ground turmeric

4 tbsp unsweetened coconut cream

1¼ cups hot Vegetable Stock
(see page 13)

3 kaffir lime leaves, finely shredded

freshly cooked jasmine rice, to serve

cook's tip

All spices give the best flavor when freshly crushed, but if you prefer, you can use ground spices instead of putting them into a mortar and crushing with a pestle.

1 Soak the cashew nuts in cold water for 8 hours, or overnight, then drain well. Seed and chop the chile. Put the coriander seeds, cumin seeds, and cardamom pods into a mortar and crush with a pestle.

2 Heat the oil in a heavy-bottomed skillet and stir-fry the onion and garlic over medium heat for 2–3 minutes to soften, but not brown. Add the chile, crushed spices, cinnamon stick, and turmeric and stir-fry for an additional 1 minute.

3 Add the coconut cream and the hot Stock to the skillet. Bring to a boil, then add the cashew nuts and lime leaves. Reduce the heat, cover, and simmer for 20 minutes. Serve hot, accompanied by freshly cooked jasmine rice.

winter vegetable cobbler

cook: 40 mins   **prep: 20 mins**   serves 4

NUTRITIONAL INFORMATION

Calories	.734
Protein	.27g
Carbohydrate	.96g
Sugars	.22g
Fat	.30g
Saturates	.16g

variation

Substitute broccoli florets for the cauliflower, or chopped turnips for the swede, if you prefer.

Seasonal fresh vegetables are casseroled with lentils then topped with a ring of fresh cheese biscuits to make this tasty cobbler.

INGREDIENTS

1 tbsp olive oil
1 garlic clove, crushed
8 small onions, halved
2 celery stalks, sliced
8 oz/225 g rutabaga, chopped
2 carrots, sliced
½ small cauliflower, broken into florets
8 oz/225 g mushrooms, sliced
14 oz/400 g canned chopped tomatoes
¼ cup red split lentils, rinsed
2 tbsp cornstarch
3–4 tbsp water
1¼ cups Vegetable Stock
(see page 13)

2 tsp Tabasco sauce
2 tsp chopped fresh oregano
fresh oregano sprigs, to garnish

TOPPING
generous 1½ cups self-rising flour
pinch of salt
4 tbsp butter
scant 1¼ cups grated mature Cheddar cheese
2 tsp chopped fresh oregano
1 egg, lightly beaten
⅔ cup milk

cook's tip

Use a biscuit cutter to cut out the dough circles, to give the edges a decorative shape. When you arrange the biscuits around the dish, make sure that you overlap them slightly.

1 Preheat the oven to 350°F/180°C. Heat the oil in a large skillet and cook the garlic and onions over low heat for 5 minutes. Add the celery, rutabaga, carrots, and cauliflower and cook for 2–3 minutes.

2 Add the mushrooms, tomatoes, and lentils. Place the cornstarch and water in a bowl and mix to make a smooth paste. Stir into the skillet with the Stock, Tabasco, and oregano. Transfer to an ovenproof dish, cover, and bake in the preheated oven for 20 minutes.

3 To make the topping, sift the flour and salt into a bowl. Rub in the butter, then stir in most of the cheese and the chopped oregano. Beat the egg with the milk in a small bowl and add enough to the dry ingredients to make a soft dough. Knead, then roll out to ½-inch/1-cm thick and cut into 2-inch/5-cm circles.

4 Remove the dish from the oven and increase the temperature to 400°F/200°C. Arrange the dough circles around the edge of the dish, brush with the remaining egg and milk mixture, and sprinkle with the reserved cheese. Cook for an additional 10–12 minutes. Garnish with oregano sprigs and serve.

cauliflower bake

serves 4　　　**prep: 10 mins** ⟳　　　**cook: 40 mins** ⟳

The bright red of the tomatoes is a great contrast to the colors of the cauliflower and herbs in this dish, making it appealing to both the eye and the palate. It is easy to prepare and satisfying to eat.

INGREDIENTS

1 lb 2 oz/500 g cauliflower, broken into florets

1 lb 5 oz/600 g potatoes, cut into cubes

3½ oz/100 g cherry tomatoes

chopped fresh flatleaf parsley, to garnish

SAUCE

2 tbsp butter or margarine

1 leek, sliced

1 garlic clove, crushed

3 tbsp all-purpose flour

1¼ cups milk

generous ¾ cup mixed grated cheese, such as Cheddar, Parmesan, and Swiss cheese

½ tsp paprika

2 tbsp chopped fresh flatleaf parsley

salt and pepper

NUTRITIONAL INFORMATION

Calories	305
Protein	. . . . .15g
Carbohydrate	. . . . .31g
Sugars	. . . . .9g
Fat	. . . . .14g
Saturates	. . . . .6g

variation

You can use broccoli instead of cauliflower for this dish, if you prefer. Alternatively, use a mixture of broccoli and cauliflower for a mix of colors.

cook's tip

When you choose a fresh cauliflower for this dish, look for a tightly packed flower with no brown marks or blemishes, surrounded by plenty of protective leaves.

1 Preheat the oven to 350°F/180°C. Cook the cauliflower florets in a pan of boiling water for 10 minutes. Meanwhile, cook the potatoes in a pan of boiling water for 10 minutes. Drain both vegetables and reserve.

2 To make the sauce, melt the butter in a large pan, add the sliced leek and garlic, and cook over low heat for 1 minute. Stir in the flour and cook, stirring constantly, for 1 minute, then remove the pan from the heat and gradually stir in the milk, ½ cup of the cheese, the paprika, and the chopped parsley. Return the pan to the heat and bring to a boil, stirring constantly. Season to taste with salt and pepper.

3 Transfer the cauliflower to a deep, ovenproof dish with the cherry tomatoes, and top with the potatoes. Pour the sauce over the potatoes and sprinkle over the remaining grated cheese.

4 Cook in the preheated oven for 20 minutes, or until the vegetables are cooked through and the cheese is golden brown and bubbling. Garnish with chopped parsley and serve.

potato-topped vegetables

 cook: 1 hr 15 mins   prep: 20 mins   serves 4

NUTRITIONAL INFORMATION	
Calories	.413
Protein	19g
Carbohydrate	.41g
Sugars	11g
Fat	18g
Saturates	11g

variation

You can parboil almost any selection of vegetables for this dish. Try stirring a handful of frozen peas into the vegetable mixture at the end of Step 2.

This is a very colorful and nutritious dish, packed full of tasty, crunchy vegetables, coated in a creamy white wine sauce.

INGREDIENTS

1 carrot, diced

6 oz/175 g cauliflower florets

6 oz/175 g broccoli florets

1 fennel bulb, sliced

3 oz/85 g green beans, halved

2 tbsp butter

2½ tbsp all-purpose flour

⅔ cup Vegetable Stock

(see page 13)

⅔ cup dry white wine

⅔ cup milk

6 oz/175 g cremini mushrooms, cut into fourths

2 tbsp chopped fresh sage

TOPPING

2 lb/900 g floury potatoes, diced

2 tbsp butter

4 tbsp plain yogurt

¾ cup freshly grated Parmesan cheese

1 tsp fennel seeds

salt and pepper

cook's tip

For an extra creamy topping, mash the potatoes with the butter and yogurt in Step 3, and before mashing in the cheese, beat the mixture for 1–2 minutes with a hand-held whisk.

1 Preheat the oven to 375°F/190°C. Cook the carrot, cauliflower, broccoli, fennel, and beans in a pan of boiling water for 10 minutes, until just tender. Drain the vegetables and reserve.

2 Melt the butter in a pan. Stir in the flour and cook over low heat for 1 minute. Remove from the heat and stir in the Stock, wine, and milk. Return to the heat and bring the mixture to a boil, stirring constantly, until thickened. Stir in the reserved vegetables, mushrooms, and chopped sage.

3 To make the topping, cook the potatoes in a pan of boiling water for 10–15 minutes. Drain and mash with the butter, yogurt, and half the cheese. Stir in the fennel seeds. Season to taste.

4 Spoon the vegetable mixture into a 4-cup pie dish. Spoon the potato mixture over the top, sprinkle over the remaining cheese, and cook in the oven for 30–35 minutes, or until golden. Serve immediately.

rice & pasta

A staple for half the world, rice is one of the most versatile of ingredients, partnering vegetables, meat, poultry, fish, and shellfish with equal ease. From Great Britain to Thailand, almost every country in the world has its own favorite rice-based dish. Most famous of all, perhaps, are Italy's risottos, and this chapter features three very different but absolutely delicious versions, with hints and tips on how to achieve the desired creamy perfection.

Pasta and noodles also play an important role in the cuisines of the world—but most are not one-pot dishes. As a general rule, pasta and sauce are cooked separately and, although recipes may be easy, there is no getting away from using several pans. Well, the exception proves the rule and this chapter includes the fabulous Pasta with Garlic & Pine Nuts (see page 195), with its delicious no-cook sauce, and the scrumptious all-in-one Crisp Noodle & Vegetable Stir-Fry (see page 200).

Some dishes are flavored with meat or fish, others are vegetarian or even vegan. Delight your guests with saffron-colored Spanish Rice with Chicken (see page 175), a mouth-watering Jambalaya (see page 184) or a luxuriously rich-tasting Risotto with Four Cheeses (see page 188). If you are in a hurry for the family supper, why not try Pork Hash (see page 180) or Pasta with Pesto (see page 202), and, if it's too hot to do much cooking, then Tricolor Pasta Salad (see page 194) is an almost instant solution.

greek chicken & rice

serves 4　　　　　**prep: 15 mins** ⏲　　　　　**cook: 40–45 mins** ♨

Look for large, slightly wrinkled Greek olives marinated in oil, and for ewe's milk feta cheese, to give this dish an authentic flavor.

INGREDIENTS

8 chicken thighs
2 tbsp corn oil
1 onion, chopped
2 garlic cloves, finely chopped
scant 1 cup long-grain rice
scant 1 cup Chicken Stock
(see page 13)
1 lb 12 oz/800 g canned
chopped tomatoes
1 tbsp chopped fresh thyme
2 tbsp chopped fresh oregano
12 black olives, pitted and chopped
2 oz/55 g feta cheese, crumbled
fresh oregano sprigs, to garnish

NUTRITIONAL INFORMATION	
Calories	.417
Protein	.25g
Carbohydrate	.47g
Sugars	.8g
Fat	.16g
Saturates	.3g

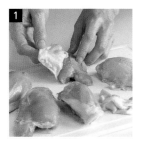

1 Remove the skin from the chicken. Heat the oil in a flameproof casserole. Add the chicken, in batches, if necessary, and cook over medium heat, turning occasionally, for 8–10 minutes, or until golden. Transfer to a plate with a perforated spoon.

2 Add the onion, garlic, long-grain rice, and a scant ¼ cup of the Stock to the casserole and cook, stirring, for 5 minutes, or until the onion is softened. Pour in the remaining Stock and add the tomatoes and their juices and the herbs.

3 Return the chicken thighs to the casserole, pushing them down into the rice. Bring to a boil, then reduce the heat, cover, and simmer for 25–30 minutes, or until the chicken is cooked through and tender. Stir in the olives and sprinkle the cheese on top. Garnish with oregano sprigs and serve immediately.

cook's tip

If you can afford organic chicken, it will have a better texture and flavor than ordinary chicken. If you are using frozen chicken, check that it is thoroughly thawed before you begin cooking.

spanish rice with chicken

⏲ **cook: 1 hr 10 mins**　　　⏱ **prep: 15 mins**　　　**serves 4**

Saffron gives this hearty, warming dish a lovely sunshine-yellow color, while mild green chiles add a kick to the flavor.

NUTRITIONAL INFORMATION	
Calories 616	
Protein 52g	
Carbohydrate 47g	
Sugars 7g	
Fat 24g	
Saturates 5g	

INGREDIENTS

3 tbsp olive oil

2 lb 12 oz/1.25 kg chicken pieces

salt and pepper

2 onions, sliced

scant 1 cup long-grain rice

½ cup dry white wine

pinch of saffron threads, lightly crushed

1½ cups Chicken Stock
(see page 13)

1–2 mild fresh green chiles,
such as serrano

2 garlic cloves, finely chopped

2 beefsteak tomatoes, peeled, seeded
and chopped

fresh cilantro sprigs, to garnish

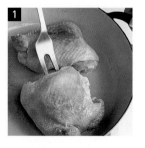

variation

For extra color, garnish the dish with 5 oz/140 g of bottled pimientos—a mild variety of pepper—cut into very thin strips.

1 Heat 2 tablespoons of the oil in a flameproof casserole. Season the chicken, add to the casserole, and cook over medium heat, turning occasionally, for 8–10 minutes, or until golden. Transfer to a plate with a perforated spoon.

2 Add the remaining oil to the casserole. Add the onions and cook over low heat, stirring occasionally, for 5 minutes, or until translucent. Add the rice and cook, stirring, for 2 minutes, or until the grains are transparent and coated with oil.

3 Pour in the wine. Bring to a boil, then reduce the heat, cover, and simmer for 8 minutes, or until all the liquid has been absorbed. Combine the saffron and Stock and pour into the casserole. Stir in the chiles and garlic and season to taste with salt. Cover and simmer for 15 minutes.

4 Add the tomatoes and return the chicken pieces to the casserole, pushing them down into the rice. Cover and cook for an additional 25 minutes, or until the chicken is cooked through and tender. Garnish with cilantro sprigs and serve.

louisiana rice

cook: 30 mins

prep: 20 mins, plus 15 mins standing

serves 4

NUTRITIONAL INFORMATION

Calories	.394
Protein	.26g
Carbohydrate	.36g
Sugars	.5g
Fat	.17g
Saturates	.3g

variation

You can substitute a small zucchini, chopped, for the celery, if you would prefer a milder flavor in this dish.

This lightly spiced, filling dish from the Deep South is quick, easy and economical—perfect for a midweek supper.

INGREDIENTS

4 tbsp corn oil

8 oz/225 g fresh ground pork

1 onion, chopped

1 garlic clove, finely chopped

1 eggplant, diced

1 green bell pepper, seeded and diced

2 celery stalks, chopped

1 tsp paprika

1 tsp cayenne pepper

1 tbsp chopped fresh thyme

salt and pepper

generous 1¾ cup Chicken Stock (see page 13)

8 oz/225 g ground chicken livers

scant ¾ cup long-grain rice

1 bay leaf

3 tbsp chopped fresh parsley

cook's tip

Rinsing uncooked rice in cold water helps to remove some of the starch. This ensures that the grains are less likely to stick together during cooking.

1 Heat the oil in a large, heavy-bottomed skillet. Add the pork and cook over medium heat, stirring, for 8–10 minutes, or until broken up and browned. Add the onion, garlic, eggplant, green bell pepper, celery, paprika, cayenne, and thyme and season to taste. Cover and cook, stirring frequently, for 5 minutes.

2 Stir in the Stock, scraping up any sediment on the bottom of the skillet. Cover and simmer for 5 minutes. Add the chicken livers and cook for 2–3 minutes. Stir in the rice and the bay leaf.

3 Cover and simmer for 7 minutes, then remove the skillet from the heat, but do not uncover. Let steam for 15 minutes, or until the rice is tender. Stir in the parsley, fluff up the rice, and serve.

chicken basquaise

serves 4   **prep: 15 mins**   **cook: 1 hr 20 mins**

Sweet bell peppers are a typical ingredient of dishes originating in the Basque region in France. In this recipe, Bayonne ham from the Pyrenees adds a delicious extra flavor.

INGREDIENTS

1 chicken, about 3 lb/1.3 kg, cut into 8 pieces	2 cups Chicken Stock (see page 13)
2 tbsp all-purpose flour	1 tsp chili flakes
salt and pepper	½ tsp dried thyme
3 tbsp olive oil	4 oz/115 g Bayonne ham, diced
1 Spanish onion, thickly sliced	12 dry-cured black olives
2 red or yellow bell peppers, seeded and cut lengthwise into thick strips	2 tbsp chopped fresh flatleaf parsley
2 garlic cloves, finely chopped	
5 oz/140 g spicy chorizo sausage, peeled and cut into ½-inch/1-cm pieces	TO GARNISH
	lemon slices
1 tbsp tomato paste	fresh flatleaf parsley sprigs
1 cup long-grain rice	

NUTRITIONAL INFORMATION

Calories	.559
Protein	.50g
Carbohydrate	.44g
Sugars	.8g
Fat	.21g
Saturates	.6g

variation

You can use any type of air-dried ham for this recipe, such as Ardennes or Westphalian ham, depending on what is available in your local delicatessen.

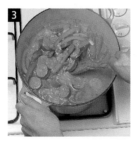

cook's tip

Browning the chicken before stewing it ensures that the meat will have an appetizing color in the finished dish. If a recipe calls for several pieces of chicken, you can brown them in batches.

1 Pat the chicken pieces dry with paper towels. Place the flour in a large plastic bag, season with salt and pepper, and add the chicken pieces. Seal the bag and shake to coat the chicken.

2 Heat 2 tablespoons of the oil in a flameproof casserole. Add the chicken and cook over medium–high heat, turning frequently, for 15 minutes, or until browned. Transfer to a plate.

3 Heat the remaining oil in the casserole and add the onion and bell peppers. Reduce the heat to medium and stir-fry until the onions color and soften. Add the garlic, chorizo, and tomato paste and cook, stirring, for 3 minutes, then add the rice and cook, stirring to coat, for 2 minutes, or until translucent.

4 Add the Stock, chili flakes, and thyme, season to taste with salt and pepper, and stir well. Bring to a boil. Return the chicken to the casserole, pressing it gently into the rice. Cover and cook over very low heat for 45 minutes, or until the chicken is cooked through and the rice is tender.

5 Gently stir the ham, olives, and half the parsley into the rice mixture. Re-cover and heat through for an additional 5 minutes. Sprinkle with the remaining parsley. Serve garnished with lemon slices and parsley sprigs.

pork hash

serves 4   **prep: 10 mins**   **cook: 55 mins**

This is a tasty dish for a midweek supper—once it's in the oven, you can put your feet up, relax with a glass of wine, and look forward to a filling meal with a feast of flavors.

INGREDIENTS

14 oz/400 g canned chopped tomatoes

2½–3 cups Beef Stock (see page 13)

1 tbsp corn oil

1 lb/450 g fresh ground pork

1 large onion, chopped

1 red bell pepper, seeded and chopped

2 cups long-grain rice

1 tbsp chili powder

1 lb/450 g fresh or frozen green beans

salt and pepper

NUTRITIONAL INFORMATION

Calories	.625
Protein	.34g
Carbohydrate	.100g
Sugars	.11g
Fat	.13g
Saturates	.3g

1 Preheat the oven to 350°F/180°C. Drain the tomatoes, reserving their juices, and reserve. Make the juices up to 3½ cups with the Stock and reserve.

2 Heat the oil in a large, flameproof casserole. Add the pork, onion, and red bell pepper and cook over medium heat, stirring frequently, for 8–10 minutes, or until the onion is softened and the meat is broken up and golden brown. Add the rice and cook, stirring constantly, for 2 minutes.

3 Add the tomatoes, stock mixture, chili powder, and beans to the casserole and season to taste with salt and pepper. Bring to a boil, then cover and transfer to the preheated oven to bake for 40 minutes. Serve immediately.

variation

For a beef hash, substitute ground beef for the pork, and if you prefer, use peas instead of beans.

tuna rice

cook: 10 mins   **prep: 10 mins**   serves 4

This is a scrumptious way to use up leftover boiled rice. Alternatively, next time you serve rice with a meal, put an extra 1¼ cups on to cook and serve this easy dish the next day.

NUTRITIONAL INFORMATION	
Calories	460
Protein	20g
Carbohydrate	66g
Sugars	1g
Fat	14g
Saturates	2g

INGREDIENTS

3 tbsp peanut or corn oil

4 scallions, chopped

2 garlic cloves, finely chopped

7 oz/200 g canned tuna in oil, drained and flaked

6 oz/175 g frozen or canned corn kernels and bell peppers

3½ cups cold boiled rice

2 tbsp Thai fish sauce

1 tbsp light soy sauce

salt and pepper

2 tbsp chopped fresh cilantro, to garnish

cook's tip

Leftover cooked rice should be cooled quickly, stored in the refrigerator, and eaten within 24 hours. It is essential that the rice is cold and dry before you stir-fry it, otherwise it will become sticky.

1 Heat the peanut oil in a preheated wok or large, heavy-bottomed skillet. Add the scallions and stir-fry for 2 minutes, then add the garlic and stir-fry for an additional 1 minute.

2 Add the tuna and the corn and bell peppers, and stir-fry for 2 minutes.

3 Add the rice, fish sauce, and soy sauce and stir-fry for 2 minutes. Season to taste with salt and pepper and serve immediately, garnished with chopped cilantro.

azerbaijani lamb pilaf

cook: 45 mins **prep: 15 mins** **serves 4**

NUTRITIONAL INFORMATION

Calories	.399
Protein	.25g
Carbohydrate	.45g
Sugars	.19g
Fat	.13g
Saturates	.4g

variation

This pilaf will work just as well with long-grain rice or basmati rice substituted for the risotto rice.

This type of dish is popular in the Balkans and through Russia to the Middle East. The saffron threads and pomegranate juice give it an exotic aroma, color, and flavor.

INGREDIENTS

2–3 tbsp vegetable oil

1 lb 7 oz/650 g boneless lamb shoulder, cut into 1-inch/2.5-cm cubes

2 onions, coarsely chopped

1 tsp ground cumin

7 oz/200 g risotto rice

1 tbsp tomato paste

1 tsp saffron threads

scant ½ cup pomegranate juice (see Cook's Tip)

scant 3½ cups lamb stock, Chicken Stock (see page 13), or water

4 oz/115 g no-soak dried apricots or prunes, halved

2 tbsp raisins

salt and pepper

2 tbsp chopped fresh mint

2 tbsp chopped fresh watercress or arugula

cook's tip

Pomegranate juice is available from Middle Eastern food stores. If you cannot find it, substitute unsweetened grape or apple juice.

1 Heat the oil in a large flameproof casserole or pan over high heat. Add the lamb, in batches, and cook over high heat, turning frequently, for 7 minutes, or until lightly browned.

2 Add the onions, reduce the heat to medium, and cook for 2 minutes, or until beginning to soften. Add the cumin and rice and cook, stirring to coat, for 2 minutes, or until the rice is translucent. Stir in the tomato paste and the saffron threads.

3 Add the pomegranate juice and stock. Bring to a boil, stirring. Stir in the apricots and raisins. Reduce the heat to low, cover, and simmer for 20–25 minutes, or until the lamb and rice are tender and all of the liquid has been absorbed.

4 Season to taste with salt and pepper, then sprinkle the chopped mint and watercress over the pilaf and serve straight from the casserole.

jambalaya

serves 6 **prep: 20 mins** **cook: 50–55 mins**

This Cajun dish is borrowed from Spain, where it originated. Its lively mixture of chicken and shrimp makes it a good dish to serve at a brunch party, instead of the more traditional kedgeree.

INGREDIENTS

2 tbsp lard

3 lb 5 oz/1.5 kg chicken pieces

2½ tbsp all-purpose flour

8 oz/225 g rindless smoked gammon, diced

1 onion, chopped

1 orange bell pepper, seeded and sliced

12 oz/350 g tomatoes, peeled and chopped

1 garlic clove, finely chopped

1 tsp chopped fresh thyme

12 jumbo shrimp, peeled

generous 1 cup long-grain rice

scant 2 cups Chicken Stock (see page 13) or water

dash of Tabasco sauce

salt and pepper

3 scallions, finely chopped

2 tbsp chopped fresh flatleaf parsley

fresh flatleaf parsley sprigs, to garnish

NUTRITIONAL INFORMATION

Calories	.570
Protein	.59g
Carbohydrate	.42g
Sugars	.3g
Fat	.20g
Saturates	.5g

variation

If you don't want to use lard in this recipe, substitute 2 tablespoons of corn oil at the beginning of Step 1.

cook's tip

Jambalaya is a Cajun dish, the idea for which originally came from Spain. If you like an even hotter taste, add 1 teaspoon of cayenne pepper with the seasoning in Step 3.

1 Melt the lard in a large, flameproof casserole. Add the chicken and cook over medium heat, turning occasionally, for 8–10 minutes, or until golden brown all over. Transfer the chicken to a plate with a perforated spoon.

2 Add the flour and cook over very low heat, stirring, for 15 minutes, or until golden brown. Do not let it burn. Return the chicken pieces to the casserole with the gammon, onion, bell pepper, tomatoes, garlic, and thyme. Cook, stirring frequently, for 10 minutes.

3 Stir in the shrimp, rice, and Stock and season to taste with Tabasco, salt, and pepper. Bring the mixture to a boil, reduce the heat, and cook for 15–20 minutes, or until all of the liquid has been absorbed and the rice is tender. Stir in the scallions and chopped parsley, garnish with parsley sprigs, and serve.

seafood risotto

cook: 30 mins   **prep: 15 mins**   **serves 4**

NUTRITIONAL INFORMATION	
Calories	.547
Protein	.46g
Carbohydrate	.60g
Sugars	.8g
Fat	.15g
Saturates	.6g

variation

You can substitute chunks of angler fish for the cod to give the dish a slightly meatier texture, if you prefer.

The secret of a successful risotto is to use round grain Italian rice, and to add a ladleful of stock at a time, making sure that the liquid is fully absorbed before more is added.

INGREDIENTS

12 oz/350 g skinless cod fillet

2 tbsp unsalted butter

1 onion, chopped

2 red bell peppers, seeded and chopped

4 tomatoes, peeled, seeded and chopped

8 ready-prepared scallops

2 tbsp olive oil

generous 1 cup risotto rice

scant 2 cups hot Fish Stock (see page 13)

salt

8 oz/225 g cooked peeled shrimp

1 tbsp chopped flatleaf parsley

2 tbsp freshly grated Parmesan cheese

fresh parsley sprigs, to garnish

cook's tip

Risotto rice will absorb stock more readily if the stock is kept at simmering point in another pan while it is being added in Step 2.

1 Cut the fish into cubes. Melt half the butter in a large pan. Add the onion, bell peppers, and tomatoes and cook over low heat, stirring occasionally, for 5 minutes, or until softened. Add the fish and scallops, and cook for an additional 3 minutes. Transfer the fish mixture to a plate with a perforated spoon, cover, and reserve.

2 Add the oil to the pan and heat gently. Add the rice and stir to coat with the butter and oil. Stir in a ladleful of Stock and season to taste with salt. Cook, stirring, until the Stock has been absorbed. Continue cooking and adding Stock, a ladleful at a time, for 20 minutes, or until the rice is tender and all of the liquid has been absorbed.

3 Gently stir in the reserved fish mixture with the shrimp and heat through for 2 minutes. Transfer the risotto to a warmed serving dish, sprinkle with the chopped parsley and Parmesan cheese, and serve immediately, garnished with parsley sprigs.

risotto with four cheeses

serves 4   **prep: 15 mins**   **cook: 30 mins**

Rich and with a subtle flavor, this is a classic Italian dish that would normally be served before the main meal.

INGREDIENTS

2 oz/55 g Taleggio cheese

2 oz/55 g Fontina cheese

2 oz/55 g Parmesan cheese

2 oz/55 g Gorgonzola cheese

3 tbsp unsalted butter

1 onion, finely chopped

scant 1⅔ cups risotto rice

generous ¾ cup dry white wine

4 cups hot Vegetable Stock
(see page 13)

salt and pepper

fresh flatleaf parsley sprigs,
to garnish

NUTRITIONAL INFORMATION	
Calories	.425
Protein	.14g
Carbohydrate	.53g
Sugars	.2g
Fat	.17g
Saturates	.11g

variation

You can use other cheeses for this risotto, but try to get a mixture of flavors. Try a combination of Swiss cheese, buffalo mozzarella, and romano.

1 Grate the Taleggio, Fontina, and Parmesan cheeses and crumble the Gorgonzola cheese, then reserve until required.

2 Melt the butter in a large pan, add the onion, and cook over low heat, stirring occasionally, for 5 minutes, or until softened. Add the rice and stir to coat the grains with butter. Add the wine and cook until almost all of it has been absorbed.

3 Add a ladleful of Stock and cook, stirring, until the liquid has been absorbed. Continue cooking and adding the Stock, a ladleful at a time, for 20 minutes, or until the rice is tender and all of the liquid has been absorbed.

4 Turn off the heat and stir in the Gorgonzola, Taleggio, Fontina, and ½ oz/ 15 g of the Parmesan cheese, until melted. Season to taste with salt and pepper. Transfer the risotto to a serving dish, sprinkle with the remaining Parmesan cheese, garnish with parsley sprigs, and serve.

risotto primavera

cook: 30 mins **prep: 10 mins** **serves 4**

As evenings get longer, the days grow warmer, and the first spring vegetables ripen, this is the ideal choice for a midweek supper.

NUTRITIONAL INFORMATION	
Calories	.399
Protein	.11g
Carbohydrate	.54g
Sugars	.4g
Fat	.16g
Saturates	.7g

INGREDIENTS

4 oz/115 g asparagus spears, cut into short lengths
2 young carrots, thinly sliced
2 tbsp unsalted butter
2 tbsp olive oil
1 white onion, chopped
2 garlic cloves, finely chopped
generous 1 cup risotto rice
3 tbsp dry white wine
4 cups hot Vegetable Stock (see page 13)
2 oz/55 g white mushrooms, halved
salt and pepper
½ cup freshly grated Parmesan cheese, to serve

cook's tip

White onions, which are very popular in Italy, are sweeter and milder than brown onions. Alternatively, you could use a red onion for this dish.

1 Blanch the asparagus and carrots in a large pan of boiling water and drain well.

2 Melt the butter with the oil in a large, heavy-bottomed pan. Add the onion and garlic and cook over low heat, stirring occasionally, for 5 minutes, or until softened. Add the rice and stir well to coat the grains with the butter and oil mixture. Add the white wine and cook until the liquid has been fully absorbed.

3 Add a ladleful of Stock to the rice and cook, stirring, until the liquid has been absorbed. Continue cooking and adding the Stock, a ladleful at a time, for 20 minutes, or until the rice is tender and all of the liquid has been absorbed.

4 Gently stir in the asparagus, carrots, and mushrooms, season to taste, and cook for an additional 2 minutes, or until heated through. Serve immediately, handing the Parmesan cheese separately.

rice & peas

serves 4   **prep: 15 mins**   **cook: 30 mins**

This is a famous dish from the Veneto region of Italy, known as Risi e Bisi. Pancetta is cured belly of pork—this is the Italian equivalent of unsmoked bacon, and it is available from some large food stores and from Italian delicatessens.

INGREDIENTS

¼ cup unsalted butter	9 oz/250 g fresh peas
1 tbsp olive oil	salt and pepper
1 red onion, chopped	scant 1 cup risotto rice
1 garlic clove, finely chopped	3 tbsp chopped fresh flatleaf parsley
2 oz/55 g pancetta, chopped	2 oz/55 g Parmesan cheese
6¼ cups Chicken Stock (see page 13)	Parmesan cheese shavings, to garnish

NUTRITIONAL INFORMATION

Calories 484

Protein 15g

Carbohydrate 52g

Sugars 4g

Fat 25g

Saturates 13g

variation

To use frozen peas, add them with the parsley in Step 3, but before adding the butter and cheese, cook for 5 minutes, until tender.

cook's tip

Try to use fresh rather than frozen peas for this recipe if at all possible. Much of the charm of the dish comes from their tenderness and freshness.

1 Melt half the butter with the olive oil in a large, heavy-bottomed pan. Add the onion, garlic, and pancetta and cook over low heat, stirring occasionally, for 5 minutes, or until the onion has softened.

2 Add the Stock and peas and season to taste with salt and pepper. Bring the mixture to a boil. Add the rice, return to a boil, then reduce the heat and simmer, stirring occasionally, for 20 minutes, or until the rice is tender. Meanwhile, grate the Parmesan cheese and reserve until required.

3 Add the parsley and stir in the remaining butter and the freshly grated Parmesan cheese. When the cheese has melted, transfer to a warmed dish, garnish with the Parmesan cheese shavings, and serve immediately.

lentil & rice casserole

serves 4 **prep: 15 mins** (b) **cook: 40 mins** (steam)

This is a really hearty dish, perfect for cold days when a substantial hot dish is just what you need to keep you warm.

INGREDIENTS

generous 1 cup red split lentils, rinsed

¼ cup long-grain rice

5 cups Vegetable Stock (see page 13)

1 leek, cut into chunks

3 garlic cloves, crushed

14 oz/400 g canned chopped tomatoes

1 tsp each of ground cumin, chili powder, and garam masala

1 red bell pepper, seeded and sliced

3½ oz/100 g small broccoli florets

8 baby corn cobs, halved lengthwise

2 oz/55 g green beans, halved

1 tbsp shredded fresh basil

salt and pepper

fresh basil sprigs, to garnish

NUTRITIONAL INFORMATION	
Calories	312
Protein	20g
Carbohydrate	51g
Sugars	9g
Fat	2g
Saturates	0.4g

variation

You can vary the rice in this recipe—instead of the long-grain rice, use brown or wild rice, if you prefer.

1 Place the lentils, rice, and Vegetable Stock in a flameproof casserole and cook over low heat, stirring occasionally, for 20 minutes.

2 Add the leek and garlic to the pan with the tomatoes and their juices,

ground spices, bell pepper, broccoli, baby corn, and green beans and stir well to mix.

3 Bring the mixture to a boil, then reduce the heat, cover, and simmer for an additional 10–15 minutes, until the vegetables are tender.

4 Add the shredded basil and season to taste with salt and pepper. Garnish with basil sprigs and serve.

linguine with tomato sauce

cook: 10 mins

prep: 10 mins, plus 30 mins marinating

serves 4

The best time to cook this dish is in the middle of summer—you should use large, sun-ripened tomatoes for the fabulous fresh sauce.

NUTRITIONAL INFORMATION

Calories	.683
Protein	.15g
Carbohydrate	.88g
Sugars	.8g
Fat	.33g
Saturates	.4g

INGREDIENTS

4 large tomatoes, peeled, seeded and diced

2 garlic cloves, finely chopped

8 fresh basil leaves, shredded

1 tbsp chopped fresh parsley

1 tbsp chopped fresh oregano

⅔ cup extra virgin olive oil

salt and pepper

1 lb/450 g dried linguine

4 oz/115 g pitted black olives, chopped

TO SERVE

baby corn salad

shredded beet

variation

You can serve any long pasta, such as spaghetti, with this sauce. If you use fresh pasta, cook for only 2–3 minutes after the water returns to a boil.

1 Place the tomatoes in a shallow, nonmetallic dish. Add the garlic, basil, parsley, oregano, and oil and season to taste with salt and pepper. Mix well, cover with plastic wrap, and let marinate for 30 minutes.

2 Bring a large pan of lightly salted water to a boil. Add the pasta, return to a boil and cook for 8–10 minutes, or until tender but still firm to the bite. Drain the pasta and return it to the pan.

3 Add the tomatoes with their marinade and the olives. Toss well and serve with baby corn salad and shredded beet.

tricolor pasta salad

serves 4　　　**prep: 10 mins** ⏱　　　**cook: 10 mins** ⏱

*This prettily colored salad is full of lovely, refreshing flavors—
tomatoes, cheese, avocado, basil, and pine nuts.*

INGREDIENTS

salt and pepper

6 oz/175 g dried fusilli

1 avocado

6 tomatoes, thinly sliced

8 oz/225 g mozzarella cheese,
thinly sliced

2 tbsp toasted pine nuts

fresh basil leaves, to garnish

DRESSING

6 tbsp extra virgin olive oil

2 tbsp white wine vinegar

1 tsp Dijon mustard

2 tbsp shredded fresh basil leaves

pinch of sugar

NUTRITIONAL INFORMATION	
Calories 593
Protein 22g
Carbohydrate 39g
Sugars 7g
Fat 40g
Saturates 12g

cook's tip

Do not peel the avocado in
advance of preparing and
serving the salad, because the
flesh quickly discolors on
exposure to the air.

1 Bring a large pan of lightly salted water to a boil. Add the pasta, return to the boil, and cook for 8–10 minutes, or until tender but still firm to the bite. Drain, refresh under cold running water, and drain again.

2 To make the dressing, whisk the oil, vinegar, mustard, basil, and sugar together in a small bowl until combined. Season to taste with salt and pepper.

3 Cut the avocado in half and remove the stone. Peel, then thinly slice the flesh lengthwise.

4 Arrange the slices of avocado, tomato, and mozzarella cheese, overlapping slightly, around the outside of a large serving platter. Add half the dressing to the pasta, toss well, then spoon into the center of the platter. Pour the remaining dressing over the salad, sprinkle with the pine nuts, garnish with basil leaves, and serve.

pasta with garlic & pine nuts

cook: 10 mins **prep: 10 mins** **serves 4**

When you are in a hurry, pasta is the answer. This tasty sauce can be prepared while the pasta is cooking to make a meal in minutes.

NUTRITIONAL INFORMATION

Calories	.397
Protein	.10g
Carbohydrate	.48g
Sugars	.3g
Fat	.20g
Saturates	.2g

INGREDIENTS

salt and pepper

9 oz/250 g dried elicoidali or penne

3 garlic cloves, coarsely chopped

2 canned anchovy fillets, drained
and coarsely chopped

2 tbsp bottled capers, drained
and finely chopped

1 tsp tarragon mustard

scant ¼ cup extra virgin olive oil

4 tbsp chopped mixed fresh herbs,
such as tarragon, chives, and
flatleaf parsley

scant ½ cup toasted pine nuts

1 tbsp lemon juice

Parmesan cheese shavings, to garnish

cook's tip

Time the pasta from the moment when the water returns to a boil and begin testing when it has been boiling for 8 minutes. Test by breaking off a small piece and biting it with your front teeth.

1 Bring a large pan of lightly salted water to a boil. Add the pasta, return to a boil, and cook for 8–10 minutes, or until tender but still firm to the bite.

2 Meanwhile, put the garlic and anchovies into a mortar and pound with a pestle to make a paste. Scrape the paste into a bowl and stir in the capers and tarragon mustard.

3 Gradually stir in the oil, then add the chopped fresh herbs, toasted pine nuts, and lemon juice and season the mixture to taste with salt and pepper.

4 Drain the pasta thoroughly and return it to the pan. Add the sauce and toss well to coat the pasta. Serve immediately, garnished with Parmesan cheese shavings.

cashew nut paella

serves 4　　　　　**prep: 15 mins** ⟳　　　　　**cook: 35 mins** ⟳

Paella traditionally contains chicken and fish, but this recipe is packed with vegetables and nuts for a truly delicious and simple vegetarian dish.

INGREDIENTS

2 tbsp olive oil

1 tbsp butter

1 red onion, chopped

generous ⅔ cup risotto rice

1 tsp ground turmeric

1 tsp ground cumin

½ tsp chili powder

3 garlic cloves, crushed

1 fresh green chile, sliced

1 green bell pepper, seeded and diced

1 red bell pepper, seeded and diced

2¾ oz/75 g baby corn cobs, halved lengthwise

2 tbsp pitted black olives

1 large tomato, seeded and diced

2 cups Vegetable Stock (see page 13)

½ cup unsalted cashew nuts

½ cup frozen peas

2 tbsp chopped fresh parsley

pinch of cayenne pepper

salt and pepper

fresh flatleaf parsley sprigs, to garnish

NUTRITIONAL INFORMATION	
Calories	.406
Protein	.10g
Carbohydrate	.44g
Sugars	.8g
Fat	.22g
Saturates	.6g

variation

Replace the cashew nuts with the same amount of roasted peanuts and use a red chile instead of green, if you prefer.

cook's tip

Always buy firm, shiny, and heavy fresh chiles. Remove the packaging and store in the refrigerator, otherwise they tend to become limp very quickly.

1 Heat the olive oil and butter in a large skillet or paella pan until the butter has melted.

2 Add the onion to the skillet and cook over medium heat, stirring constantly, for 2–3 minutes, or until the onion has softened.

3 Stir in the rice, turmeric, ground cumin, chili powder, garlic, sliced chile, bell peppers, baby corn, black olives, and diced tomato and cook over medium heat, stirring occasionally, for 1–2 minutes.

4 Pour in the Vegetable Stock and bring the mixture to a boil. Reduce the heat and cook, stirring constantly, for 20 minutes.

5 Add the cashew nuts and peas and cook, stirring occasionally, for 5 minutes. Season to taste with salt and pepper and sprinkle with chopped parsley and cayenne pepper. Transfer to serving plates, garnish with parsley sprigs, and serve.

vegetable lasagna

cook: 55 mins   **prep: 15 mins, plus 20 mins standing**   **serves 4**

variation

Substitute blanched, bite-size lengths of asparagus spears for the celery stalks, for a slightly different flavor.

This colorful and tasty lasagna has layers of vegetables in tomato sauce and eggplants, all topped with a rich cheese sauce.

INGREDIENTS

1 large eggplant, sliced

salt and pepper

3 tbsp olive oil

2 garlic cloves, crushed

1 red onion, halved and sliced

3 mixed bell peppers, seeded and diced

8 oz/225 g mixed mushrooms, sliced

2 celery stalks, sliced

1 zucchini, diced

½ tsp chili powder

½ tsp ground cumin

2 tomatoes, chopped

1¼ cups strained tomatoes

2 tbsp chopped fresh basil

8 no-pre-cook lasagna verdi sheets

CHEESE SAUCE

2 tbsp butter or margarine

1 tbsp all-purpose flour

⅔ cup Vegetable Stock (see page 13)

1¼ cups milk

¾ cup grated Cheddar cheese

1 tsp Dijon mustard

1 tbsp chopped fresh basil

1 egg, beaten

cook's tip

Dijon mustard is one of the best types to use for a cheese sauce. It is a very hot mustard, and its heat brings out the flavor of the cheese.

1 Preheat the oven to 350°F/180°C. Place the eggplant slices in a colander, sprinkle with salt, and let stand for 20 minutes. Rinse under cold running water, drain, and reserve until required.

2 Heat the oil in a skillet. Add the garlic and onion and cook over medium heat for

1–2 minutes. Add the bell peppers, mushrooms, celery, and zucchini and cook, stirring constantly, for an additional 3–4 minutes.

3 Stir in the spices and cook for 1 minute. Stir in the chopped tomatoes, strained tomatoes, and basil and season the mixture to taste with salt and pepper.

4 To make the sauce, melt the butter in a pan, stir in the flour, and cook for 1 minute. Remove from the heat, stir in the Stock and milk, then return to the heat and stir in half the cheese and the mustard. Bring the sauce to a boil, stirring, until thickened. Stir in the basil, then remove from the heat and stir in the egg.

5 Place half the lasagna sheets in an ovenproof dish. Top with half the vegetable mixture, then half the eggplant slices. Repeat the layers and spoon the cheese sauce over the top. Sprinkle the lasagna with the remaining cheese and cook in the preheated oven for 40 minutes, or until the topping is golden. Serve immediately.

crisp noodle & vegetable stir-fry

serves 4 **prep: 5 mins** ↺ **cook: 15–20 mins** ⏲

Once you have chopped the vegetables, this dish is quick and easy to put together, and makes an attractive and nutritious meal for the family, or for visitors expecting a bite to eat.

INGREDIENTS

peanut or corn oil, for deep-frying

4 oz/115 g rice vermicelli, broken into 3-inch/7.5-cm lengths

4 oz/115 g green beans, cut into short lengths

2 carrots, cut into thin sticks

2 zucchini, cut into thin sticks

4 oz/115 g shiitake mushrooms, sliced

1-inch/2.5-cm piece fresh gingerroot, shredded

½ small head Napa cabbage, shredded

4 scallions, shredded

generous ¾ cup bean sprouts

2 tbsp dark soy sauce

2 tbsp Chinese rice wine

large pinch of sugar

2 tbsp coarsely chopped fresh cilantro

NUTRITIONAL INFORMATION

Calories	240
Protein	7g
Carbohydrate	33g
Sugars	6g
Fat	9g
Saturates	1g

variation

For a spicier version of this dish, add 1 seeded and sliced fresh red chile with the gingerroot in Step 2.

cook's tip

This dish also looks attractive if you serve the noodles in a small nest on top of the stir-fried vegetables, rather than tossing them with the vegetables in Step 3.

1 Half-fill a preheated wok or deep, heavy-bottomed skillet with oil. Heat to 350–375°F/180–190°C, or until a cube of bread browns in 30 seconds. Add the noodles, in batches, and cook for 1½–2 minutes, or until crisp and puffed up. Remove and drain on paper towels. Pour off all but 2 tablespoons of oil from the wok.

2 Heat the remaining oil over high heat, then add the green beans and stir-fry for 2 minutes. Add the carrot and zucchini sticks, sliced mushrooms, and gingerroot and stir-fry for an additional 2 minutes. Add the shredded Napa cabbage and scallions with the bean sprouts and stir-fry for an additional 1 minute.

3 Add the soy sauce, Chinese rice wine, and sugar and cook, stirring constantly, for 1 minute. Add the noodles and chopped cilantro and toss well. Serve immediately.

pasta with pesto

serves 4   **prep: 10–15 mins** ⏲   **cook: 10 mins** ⏲

Traditionally, the Genoese make this delicious sauce with a pestle and mortar. The taste of this fresh version will be a revelation.

INGREDIENTS

salt

1 lb/450 g dried tagliatelle

fresh basil sprigs, to garnish

PESTO

2 garlic cloves

scant ¼ cup pine nuts

sea salt

4 oz/115 g fresh basil leaves

½ cup olive oil

½ cup freshly grated Parmesan cheese

NUTRITIONAL INFORMATION	
Calories 705	
Protein 21g	
Carbohydrate 85g	
Sugars 4g	
Fat 34g	
Saturates 6g	

cook's tip

To store pesto, place it in a screw-top jar, cover the surface with a layer of olive oil, and keep in the refrigerator for up to 1 month.

1 To make the pesto, place the garlic, pine nuts, and a large pinch of sea salt in a blender or food processor and process briefly. Add the basil leaves and process to a paste.

2 With the motor running, gradually add the oil. Scrape into a bowl and beat in the cheese. Season to taste with salt. Alternatively, put the garlic, pine nuts, a large pinch of sea salt, and the basil leaves into a mortar and crush with a pestle to make a paste. Transfer to a bowl, work in the Parmesan cheese, then gradually add the oil, beating with a wooden spoon. Season to taste with salt.

3 Bring a large pan of lightly salted water to a boil. Add the pasta, return to a boil, and cook for 8–10 minutes, or until tender but still firm to the bite. Drain well, return to the pan and toss with half the pesto, then divide between warmed serving plates and top with the remaining pesto. Garnish with basil sprigs and serve.

macaroni cheese & tomato

cook: 35–50 mins　　　**prep: 15 mins**　　　**serves 4**

This is a really simple, family dish which is inexpensive and easy to prepare and cook. Serve with a salad or fresh green vegetables.

NUTRITIONAL INFORMATION

Calories 592

Protein 28g

Carbohydrate 57g

Sugars 6g

Fat 29g

Saturates 17g

INGREDIENTS

2¼ cups dried elbow macaroni

1¾ cups grated Cheddar cheese

1 cup grated Parmesan cheese

4 tbsp fresh white bread crumbs

1 tbsp chopped fresh basil

1 tbsp butter, plus extra for greasing

TOMATO SAUCE

1 tbsp olive oil

1 shallot, finely chopped

2 garlic cloves, crushed

1 lb 2 oz/500 g canned tomatoes

1 tbsp chopped fresh basil

salt and pepper

variation

Substitute the macaroni with 8 oz/225 g dried penne or fusilli and use whole-wheat bread crumbs instead of white.

1 Preheat the oven to 375°F/190°C. To make the tomato sauce, heat the oil in a heavy-bottomed pan. Add the shallots and garlic and cook for 1 minute. Add the tomatoes and basil and season to taste with salt and pepper. Cook over medium heat, stirring constantly, for 10 minutes.

2 Meanwhile, bring a large pan of lightly salted water to a boil. Add the macaroni and cook for 8 minutes, or until tender but still firm to the bite. Drain thoroughly and reserve.

3 Mix the cheeses together in a bowl. Grease a deep, ovenproof dish. Spoon one-third of the tomato sauce into the bottom of the dish, top with one-third of the macaroni, and then one-third of the cheeses. Season to taste with salt and pepper. Repeat these layers twice, ending with a layer of cheese.

4 Mix the bread crumbs and basil together and sprinkle evenly over the top. Dot the topping with butter and cook in the preheated oven for 25 minutes, until the topping is golden brown and bubbling. Serve immediately.

italian fish stew

cook: 25 mins   **prep: 5–10 mins**   **serves 4**

NUTRITIONAL INFORMATION

Calories	236
Protein	. . . . .20g
Carbohydrate	. . . . .25g
Sugars	. . . . .4g
Fat	. . . . .7g
Saturates	. . . . .1g

variation

Substitute 1 tablespoon chopped fresh oregano or 1 teaspoon dried oregano for the chopped basil, if you prefer, and garnish the dish with fresh oregano.

This robust stew is full of Mediterranean flavors. The firm white fish will keep its shape when cooked, making the dish look filling and appetizing—perfect for a warming meal on a chilly evening.

INGREDIENTS

2 tbsp olive oil

2 red onions, finely chopped

1 garlic clove, crushed

2 zucchini, sliced

14 oz/400 g canned chopped tomatoes

scant 3½ cups Fish or Vegetable Stock (see page 13)

3 oz/85 g dried pasta shapes

1 tbsp chopped fresh basil

1 tsp grated lemon rind

12 oz/350 g firm, skinless white fish fillets, such as cod, haddock, or hake, cut into chunks

1 tbsp cornstarch

1 tbsp water

salt and pepper

fresh basil sprigs, to garnish

cook's tip

Make sure that the fish fillets are free of bones by running your fingers over them to feel for anything sharp and removing any bones with a pair of tweezers.

1 Heat the oil in a large pan. Add the onions and garlic and cook over low heat, stirring occasionally, for 5 minutes, or until softened. Add the zucchini and cook, stirring frequently, for 2–3 minutes.

2 Add the tomatoes and Stock to the pan and bring to a boil. Add the pasta.

Return to a boil, then reduce the heat, cover, and simmer for 5 minutes.

3 Add the basil, lemon rind, and fish chunks to the pan and simmer for 5 minutes, or until the fish is cooked and flakes easily when tested with the point of a knife, and the pasta is tender but still firm to the bite.

4 Blend the cornstarch with the water to make a smooth paste and stir into the stew. Cook gently for 2 minutes, stirring constantly, until thickened. Season to taste with salt and pepper.

5 Ladle the stew into 4 warmed soup bowls. Garnish with basil sprigs and serve immediately.

seafood lasagna

serves 4 | **prep: 30 mins,** plus 10 mins standing | **cook: 1 hr 10 mins**

A rich dish of layers of pasta, with seafood and mushrooms in a tomato sauce, topped with béchamel sauce and baked until golden.

INGREDIENTS

3½ tbsp butter, plus extra for greasing

5 tbsp all-purpose flour

1 tsp mustard powder

2½ cups milk

2 tbsp olive oil

1 onion, chopped

2 garlic cloves, finely chopped

1 lb/450 g mixed mushrooms, sliced

⅔ cup white wine

14 oz/400 g canned chopped tomatoes

salt and pepper

1 lb/450 g skinless white fish fillets

8 oz/225 g ready-prepared fresh scallops

4–6 sheets fresh lasagna

8 oz/225 g mozzarella cheese, chopped

NUTRITIONAL INFORMATION	
Calories 696	
Protein 58g	
Carbohydrate 38g	
Sugars 14g	
Fat 33g	
Saturates 3g	

cook's tip

For the best consistency and flavor, it is best to buy fresh pasta from an Italian delicatessen where it is made on the premises, rather than from a large food store.

1 Preheat the oven to 400°F/200°C. Melt the butter in a pan over low heat. Add the flour and mustard powder and stir until smooth. Simmer gently for 2 minutes without coloring. Gradually add the milk, whisking until smooth. Bring to a the boil, reduce the heat, and simmer for 2 minutes. Remove from the heat and reserve. Cover the surface of the sauce with plastic wrap to prevent a skin forming.

2 Heat the oil in a skillet. Add the onion and garlic and cook gently for 5 minutes, or until softened. Add the mushrooms and cook for 5 minutes, or until softened. Stir in the wine and boil rapidly until almost evaporated, then stir in the tomatoes. Bring to a boil, reduce the heat, and simmer, covered, for 15 minutes. Season and reserve.

3 Cut the fish into cubes. Grease a lasagna dish, spoon half the tomato mixture over the bottom, top with half the fish and scallops, and layer half the lasagna over the top. Pour over half the white sauce and sprinkle over half the mozzarella. Repeat these layers, finishing with sauce and mozzarella.

4 Bake in the preheated oven for 35–40 minutes, or until golden and the fish is cooked through. Remove from the oven and let stand for 10 minutes before serving.

seafood spaghetti

cook: 30 mins   **prep: 20 mins**   **serves 4**

You can use whatever combination of shellfish you like in this recipe—it is served with freshly cooked spaghetti.

NUTRITIONAL INFORMATION

Calories	372
Protein	33g
Carbohydrate	45g
Sugars	3g
Fat	5g
Saturates	1g

INGREDIENTS

1 lb/450 g fresh mussels

8 oz/225 g baby squid

8 oz/225 g fresh prawns

8 small cooked crab claws

2 tsp olive oil

1 small red onion, finely chopped

1 tbsp lemon juice

1 garlic clove, crushed

2 celery stalks, finely chopped

⅔ cup Fish Stock (see page 13)

⅔ cup dry white wine

small bunch of fresh tarragon

8 oz/225 g dried spaghetti

salt and pepper

2 tbsp chopped fresh tarragon, to garnish

cook's tip

Crab claws contain lean crabmeat. If you can, ask your fishmonger to crack the claws for you, leaving the pincers intact, because the shell is very tough.

1 Prepare the mussels and the squid (see page 132), peel and devein the shrimp, and crack and peel the cooked crab claws. Reserve the seafood.

2 Heat the oil in a large pan. Add the onion, lemon juice, garlic, and celery and cook for 3–4 minutes, or until softened.

3 Pour in the Stock and wine. Bring to a boil and add the tarragon and mussels. Cover and simmer for 5 minutes. Add the shrimp, squid, and crab claws, stir, and cook for 3–4 minutes, or until the mussels have opened, the shrimp are pink, and the squid is opaque. Remove and discard the tarragon and any mussels that have not opened.

4 Meanwhile, bring a large pan of water to a boil. Add the pasta, return to the boil and cook for 10 minutes, or until tender but still firm to the bite. Drain well, add it to the shellfish mixture, and toss together, then season to taste with salt and pepper.

5 Transfer the spaghetti to warmed serving plates and spoon over the cooking juices. Garnish with chopped tarragon and serve.

desserts

For many cooks, dessert is one course too far, but for many diners, it is a fine finale to a meal. Compromise with this delightful selection of one-pot sweet dishes. Why bother with a conventional—and boring—fruit pie when, with far less effort and washing-up, you could make Clafoutis (see page 243), a melt-in-the-mouth combination of succulent cherries and crispy batter, or Tarte Tatin (see page 216), an all-in-one upside-down apple pie?

Whatever the season and whatever the occasion, you will find the perfect dish to round off your meal—whether an alfresco lunch, a midwinter supper, or a sophisticated dinner party. There are lots of child-friendly treats for family suppers, from Cinnamon & Apricot Crêpes (see page 245) to Apple Fritters (see page 249), as well as some delicious dishes for the more adult palate, from Syllabub (see page 232) to liqueur-laced Saucy Ice Creams (see page 253). Fruit features in many forms—hot Flambéed Peaches (see page 233) contrast with ice-cold Forest Fruits Granita (see page 251), with Warm Fruit Compote (see page 242) somewhere in between.

There are also recipes for traditional, familiar, and well-loved desserts, such as Creamed Rice (see page 219) and Zabaglione (see page 230). There are light-as-air confections and substantial desserts, to make sure that even the heartiest appetite is finally satisfied.

minted pears

serves 4

prep: 10 mins, plus 1–2 hrs cooling/chilling

cook: 35–40 mins

These sweet pears are straightforward to make and taste delicious. They can be made in advance and left to chill, making them an ideal, easy dessert after a more complex main meal.

INGREDIENTS

4 large pears

4 tbsp superfine sugar

4 tbsp clear honey

2 tbsp green crème de menthe

fresh mint sprigs, to decorate

NUTRITIONAL INFORMATION

Calories	.250
Protein	.1g
Carbohydrate	.62g
Sugars	.62g
Fat	.0g
Saturates	.0g

cook's tip

Choose firm, ripe pears that will hold their shape when poached, and leave the stems intact when peeling for an attractive finished dish.

1 Peel the pears and stand them upright in a heavy-bottomed pan. Add enough water to cover. Bring to a boil, then reduce the heat, cover, and simmer for 25–30 minutes, or until the pears are tender. Pour away half the cooking water, then add the superfine sugar to the pan and simmer for an additional 10 minutes.

2 Transfer the pears to a bowl with a perforated spoon. Pour ⅔ cup of the cooking water into a pitcher and stir in the honey and crème de menthe. Pour the syrup over the pears.

3 Set the pears aside to cool, then cover with plastic wrap and chill in the refrigerator for 1–2 hours.

Transfer the pears to individual serving bowls, spoon the mint syrup over them, and serve, decorated with fresh mint.

spun sugar pears

⏲ **cook: 40 mins**   🕗 **prep: 20 mins, plus 20 mins cooling**   **serves 4**

Whole pears poached in a Madeira syrup, then served inside a delicate case of spun sugar, make a stunningly attractive dessert, which is bound to cause a stir at any dinner party.

NUTRITIONAL INFORMATION	
Calories	166
Protein	0.3g
Carbohydrate	41g
Sugars	41g
Fat	0g
Saturates	0g

INGREDIENTS

⅔ **cup water**

⅔ **cup sweet Madeira wine**

generous ½ cup superfine sugar

2 tbsp lime juice

4 ripe pears

fresh mint sprigs, to decorate

SPUN SUGAR

generous ½ cup superfine sugar

3 tbsp water

cook's tip

The caramelized sugar stiffens slightly when it is allowed to stand after cooking. This should make it easier to handle when you spin it around the pear. Work quickly, from the bottom of the pear upwards.

1 Mix the water, Madeira, sugar, and lime juice in a deep flameproof dish or large pan. Cook over high heat for 3 minutes, stirring, until the sugar dissolves.

2 Peel the pears and cut a thin slice from the bottom of each, so that they stand upright. Place them in the dish and spoon the wine syrup over them. Cover, bring to a boil, then reduce the heat and simmer for 10 minutes, or until the pears are tender, turning them over occasionally. Cover the pears and syrup and let cool.

3 Remove the cooled pears from the syrup and place on serving plates. Bring the syrup to a boil, uncovered, then reduce the heat and simmer for 15 minutes, or until reduced by half and thickened slightly. Let stand for 5 minutes, then spoon over the pears.

4 To make the spun sugar, place the sugar and water in a small pan and cook over high heat for 6–7 minutes, stirring constantly, until the sugar has dissolved and caramelized. Let stand for 2 minutes.

5 Dip a teaspoon in the caramel and spin around each pear in a circular motion. Decorate with mint and serve.

exotic fruit pockets

🍳 cook: 15–20 mins

⏲ prep: 10 mins,
plus 30 mins marinating

serves 4

NUTRITIONAL INFORMATION	
Calories	.43
Protein	.2g
Carbohydrate	.9g
Sugars	.9g
Fat	.0.3g
Saturates	.0.1g

Delicious pieces of fresh exotic fruit are warmed through in a
scented sauce to make this fabulous grilled dessert. Silver foil
pockets and sliced carambola add a touch of glamour.

INGREDIENTS

1 papaya	3 tbsp orange juice
1 mango	light cream or lowfat
1 carambola	plain yogurt, to serve
1 tbsp grenadine	

variation

Grenadine is a sweet syrup made
from pomegranates. If you prefer you
could use pomegranate juice instead
(see Cook's Tip).

cook's tip

To extract the juice from a
pomegranate for the variation
on this recipe, cut the fruit in
half and squeeze gently with
a lemon squeezer—do not
press too hard or the juice
may become bitter.

1 Preheat the barbecue.
Cut the papaya in half,
scoop out the seeds, and
discard them. Peel the papaya
and cut the flesh into
thick slices.

2 Slice the mango in half
lengthwise around the
flat pit, then cut the flesh
carefully away from the pit.
Score each mango half in a
criss-cross pattern. Push each
half inside-out to separate the
cubes, then cut them away
from the peel.

3 Slice the carambola
thickly. Place it in a bowl
with the papaya and mango
and mix. Stir the grenadine
and orange juice together,
pour over the fruit, and let
marinate for 30 minutes.

4 Divide the marinaded
fruit between
4 double-thickness squares
of foil. Gather up the edges
to enclose the fruit in pockets.

5 Place the foil pockets
on a barbecue grill set
over warm coals and grill for
15–20 minutes. Serve in the
foil, handing the cream or
yogurt separately.

banana empanadas

serves 4   **prep: 10 mins** ⏲   **cook: 15 mins** ⏲

Using delicate phyllo pastry makes these empanadas light and crispy on the outside, while the filling inside slowly melts into a scrumptious hot banana and chocolate mixture.

INGREDIENTS

about 8 sheets of phyllo pastry,
cut in half lengthwise

melted butter or vegetable oil,
for brushing

2 ripe, sweet bananas

1–2 tsp sugar

juice of ½ lemon

6–7 oz/175–200 g semisweet chocolate,
broken into small pieces

confectioners' sugar and ground
cinnamon, for dusting

NUTRITIONAL INFORMATION	
Calories 375	
Protein 5g	
Carbohydrate 57g	
Sugars 41g	
Fat 16g	
Saturates 8g	

cook's tip

For a light and puffy effect, you could enclose the filling in sheets of ready-made puff pastry instead of phyllo, and bake in the same way.

1 Preheat the oven to 375°F/190°C. Lay out a long rectangular sheet of phyllo on a clean counter and brush with melted butter.

2 Peel and dice the bananas and place in a bowl. Add the sugar and lemon juice and stir well to blend, then stir in the chocolate. Place 2 teaspoons of the banana and chocolate mixture in one corner of the sheet of pastry, then fold over into a triangle shape to enclose the filling. Continue to fold in a triangular shape until the phyllo is wrapped around the filling. Dust the empanada with confectioners' sugar and cinnamon and place on a large cookie sheet.

3 Repeat the process with the remaining sheets of phyllo and filling.

4 Bake in the preheated oven for 15 minutes, or until the pastries are golden. Remove from the oven, serve immediately, and eat with care—the filling will be hot.

sopaipillas

cook: 15 mins　　　　**prep: 15 mins**　　　　serves 6

These little, deep-fried puffs are popular sweet snacks in Mexico. You can serve them with honey, syrup, or simply sprinkled with a mixture of sugar and ground cinnamon.

NUTRITIONAL INFORMATION	
Calories	.268
Protein	.4g
Carbohydrate	.50g
Sugars	.21g
Fat	.8g
Saturates	.1g

INGREDIENTS

generous 1½ cups all-purpose flour,
plus extra for dusting

1 tbsp baking powder

pinch of salt

2 tbsp margarine, diced

¾ cup water

corn oil, for deep-frying

runny honey, to serve

cook's tip

Make sure that the oil heats up to its original temperature again after you have cooked one batch of sopaipillas, before adding the next.

1 Sift the flour, baking powder, and salt into a bowl. Add the margarine and rub it in until the mixture resembles bread crumbs. Gradually stir in the water and bring together to make a soft dough.

2 Turn out the dough on to a lightly floured counter and knead gently until smooth. Roll out into a large, thin rectangle, then cut into 3-inch/7.5-cm squares.

3 Heat the oil in a large, deep skillet to 350–375°F/180–190°C, or until a cube of bread browns in 30 seconds. Add the dough squares and cook in batches, until puffed up and golden, turning over to cook both sides. Remove the sopaipillas with a perforated spoon and drain well on paper towels.

4 Serve the sopaipillas warm, drizzled with a little honey.

tarte tatin

serves 8 **prep: 15 mins,** plus 10 mins cooling **cook: 1 hr 5 mins**

This upside-down apple tart has been a speciality of Sologne in the Loire valley for centuries, but was made famous by the Tatin sisters who ran a hotel-restaurant in Lamotte-Beuvron at the beginning of the twentieth century.

INGREDIENTS

8 oz/225 g unsweetened pastry, thawed if frozen

all-purpose flour, for dusting

10 eating apples, such as Golden Delicious

4 tbsp lemon juice

½ cup unsalted butter, diced

generous ½ cup superfine sugar

½ tsp ground cinnamon

NUTRITIONAL INFORMATION	
Calories	348
Protein	2g
Carbohydrate	43g
Sugars	30g
Fat	20g
Saturates	11g

variation

If you can't find any Golden Delicious apples, Braeburn apples will work just as well for this traditional French tart.

cook's tip

To achieve the best decorative effect when the tart is turned over, pack the halved apples in the tin with their cut sides facing up in Step 3.

1 Preheat the oven to 450°F/230°C. Roll out the pastry on a lightly floured counter into a ¼-inch/5-mm thick circle, about 11 inches/28 cm in diameter. Transfer to a lightly floured cookie sheet and let chill in the refrigerator.

2 Peel, halve, and core the apples, then brush with the lemon juice to prevent any discoloration. Heat the butter, sugar, and cinnamon in a 10-inch/25-cm tarte tatin pan or heavy-bottomed skillet with a flameproof handle over low heat, stirring occasionally, until the butter has melted and the sugar has dissolved. Cook for an additional 6–8 minutes, or until a light caramel color, then remove from the heat.

3 Arrange the apples in the pan or skillet, packing them in tightly. Return to the heat and cook for 25 minutes, or until the apples are tender and lightly colored. Remove from the heat and let cool slightly.

4 Place the pastry over the apples, tucking in the edges. Prick the top and bake in the preheated oven for 30 minutes, or until golden. Let cool slightly, then run a knife around the edge of the pan to loosen the pastry. Invert on to a plate and serve warm.

teacup cake

This is such an easy dessert to make, because all the ingredients, except the allspice, can be measured in the same cup. It tastes best served with a generous helping of warmed custard.

INGREDIENTS

butter, for greasing
1 cup self-rising flour
1 tsp allspice
1 cup soft brown sugar
1 cup shredded suet
1 cup currants
1 cup milk
custard, to serve

NUTRITIONAL INFORMATION	
Calories . . . . .517 (per portion)	
Protein 5g	
Carbohydrate 72g	
Sugars 46g	
Fat 25g	
Saturates 14g	

1. Grease a 4-cup ovenproof bowl with butter. Sift the flour and allspice into a bowl and stir in the sugar, suet, and currants, then add the milk and mix well. Spoon the mixture into the prepared bowl.

2. Cut out a circle of waxed paper and a circle of foil 3 inches/7.5 cm larger than the rim of the bowl. Place the paper circle on top of the foil circle, grease it, and pleat both circles across the center. Place them over the bowl, paper-side down, and tie around the rim with string.

3. Place the bowl on a trivet in a large pan and fill with boiling water to come halfway up the sides. Alternatively, place it in a steamer over a pan of boiling water. Steam for 3 hours, then carefully remove from the pan. Discard the covering, turn out on to a warmed serving dish, and serve with custard.

cook's tip

It doesn't matter whether you use a standard measuring cup or an ordinary teacup to measure the ingredients, because the proportions remain the same.

creamed rice

⏱ **cook: 1 hr 5 mins**   ⏱ **prep: 5 mins**   **serves 4**

This rich, creamy dessert is a really comforting treat on cold winter days. You can serve it with a helping of canned or stewed fruit, or just enjoy it on its own.

NUTRITIONAL INFORMATION	
Calories	.405
Protein	.10g
Carbohydrate	.73g
Sugars	.42g
Fat	.10g
Saturates	.6g

INGREDIENTS

⅔ cup short-grain rice

4 cups milk

generous ½ cup sugar

1 tsp vanilla extract

TO DECORATE

ground cinnamon

cinnamon sticks

variation

For an orange flavor, omit the sugar and vanilla and stir 3 tablespoons of clear honey and the finely grated rind of 1 orange into the milk in Step 1.

1 Rinse the rice well under cold running water and drain. Pour the milk into a large, heavy-bottomed pan, add the sugar, and bring to a boil, stirring.

2 Add the rice, reduce the heat, cover, and simmer gently, stirring occasionally, for 1 hour, or until the milk has been absorbed.

3 Stir in the vanilla extract. Transfer the rice to tall, heatproof glasses, sprinkle with a light dusting of ground cinnamon, and serve immediately, decorated with cinnamon sticks.

bread & butter pudding

⏲ **cook: 50–60 mins**

⏱ **prep: 15 mins, plus 20–30 mins standing (optional)**

serves 6

NUTRITIONAL INFORMATION	
Calories 427	
Protein 9g	
Carbohydrate 74g	
Sugars 63g	
Fat 13g	
Saturates 7g	

Everyone has their own favorite recipe for this traditional English dish. This fruity version has added marmalade and grated apples to give the dessert a really rich and unique taste.

INGREDIENTS

5 tbsp butter, softened, plus extra for greasing

4–5 slices white or brown bread

4 tbsp chunky orange marmalade

grated rind of 1 lemon

½–¾ cup raisins

scant ¼ cup chopped candied peel

1 tsp ground cinnamon

1 tart cooking apple, peeled, cored, and coarsely grated

scant ½ cup light brown sugar

3 eggs

generous 2 cups milk

2 tbsp raw brown sugar

variation

You can substitute golden raisins for the raisins, and allspice for the ground cinnamon, if you prefer.

cook's tip

This dessert can be left in the dish to cool completely before serving, if you wish—it tastes just as delicious served cold, with a helping of light cream.

1 Preheat the oven to 400°F/200°C. Lightly grease an ovenproof dish with butter. Spread the slices of bread with butter, then spread the bread with marmalade.

2 Place a layer of bread in the bottom of the dish and sprinkle with the lemon rind, half the raisins, half the candied peel, half the cinnamon, all of the apple, and half the light brown sugar.

3 Add another layer of bread, cutting the slices so that they fit the dish.

4 Sprinkle over most of the remaining raisins and the remaining candied peel, cinnamon, and light brown sugar, sprinkling it evenly over the bread. Top with a final layer of bread, again cutting to fit the dish.

5 Lightly beat the eggs and milk together in a bowl, then strain the mixture over the bread in the dish. If you have enough time to spare, let the dessert stand for 20–30 minutes.

6 Sprinkle the top of the dessert with raw brown sugar and sprinkle over the remaining raisins. Cook in the preheated oven for 50–60 minutes, or until risen and golden. Serve.

fall fruit delight

prep: 10 mins, ⏲ cook: 10 mins ⏲
plus 8 hrs chilling

This is like a summer pudding, but it uses a selection of fruits, which are in season later in the year, such as apples, pears, and blackberries, to make a succulent, sweet filling.

INGREDIENTS

2 lb/900 g mixed blackberries, chopped apples, and chopped pears

¾ cup soft light brown sugar

1 tsp ground cinnamon

scant ½ cup water

8 oz/225 g white bread, thinly sliced, crusts removed

NUTRITIONAL INFORMATION	
Calories	178
Protein	3g
Carbohydrate	42g
Sugars	31g
Fat	1g
Saturates	0.1g

variation

Try using thin slices of plain sponge cake instead of the bread. The sponge will turn an attractive pinkish color from the fruit juices.

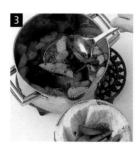

cook's tip

Stand the dessert on a plate when chilling in the refrigerator—this will catch any juices that run down the sides of the bowl.

1 Place the prepared fruit in a large pan with the sugar, cinnamon, and water. Bring to a boil, stirring, then reduce the heat and simmer for 5–10 minutes, or until the fruits soften but still hold their shape.

2 Meanwhile, line the bottom and sides of a 3½-cup ovenproof bowl with the bread slices, ensuring that there are no gaps between the pieces of bread.

3 Spoon the fruit into the center of the bread-lined bowl and cover the fruit with the remaining bread.

4 Place a saucer on top of the bread to weigh it down. Chill the dessert in the refrigerator for 8 hours, or overnight, then turn out on to a serving plate and serve.

chocolate fondue

serves 4　　　　　**prep: 15 mins**　　　　　**cook: 5 mins**

This is a fun dessert to serve at the end of an informal meal. The fondue sauce can be prepared in advance, if you like, then warmed through and transferred into the fondue dish before serving.

INGREDIENTS

8 oz/225 g semisweet chocolate
generous ¾ cup heavy cream
2 tbsp brandy

TO SERVE

selection of fresh fruit
white and pink marshmallows
sweet cookies

NUTRITIONAL INFORMATION	
Calories . . . . .536 (per portion)	
Protein 4g	
Carbohydrate 38g	
Sugars 35g	
Fat 40g	
Saturates 25g	

variation

Choose your favorite fruit to dip in the fondue. Kiwi fruit, banana chunks, apple pieces, and strawberries go particularly well.

cook's tip

To prepare the fruit for dipping, cut larger fruit into bite-size pieces. Fruit that discolors, such as bananas, apples, and pears, should be dipped in a little lemon juice as soon as it is cut.

1 Break the chocolate into small pieces and place in a small pan with the cream. Heat the mixture gently, stirring constantly, until the chocolate has melted and blended with the cream.

2 Remove the pan from the heat and stir in the brandy.

3 Pour the mixture into a fondue pot or small flameproof dish and keep warm over a small burner.

4 Serve with a selection of fruit, marshmallows, and cookies for dipping. The fruit and marshmallows can be spiked on fondue forks, wooden skewers, or ordinary forks for dipping into the chocolate fondue.

chocolate chip brownies

cook: 30–35 mins

prep: 25 mins, plus 30 mins cooling

makes 12

NUTRITIONAL INFORMATION	
Calories . . . .414 (per brownie)	
Protein 6g	
Carbohydrate 39g	
Sugars 24g	
Fat 27g	
Saturates 14g	

variation

For extra flavor, stir in ½ teaspoon of vanilla extract when you add the nuts and white chocolate in Step 4.

Choose a good quality semisweet chocolate containing 70 percent cocoa solids for these chocolate chip brownies. This will give them a rich flavor that is not overwhelmingly sweet.

INGREDIENTS

1 cup butter, softened, plus extra for greasing

5½ oz/150 g semisweet chocolate, broken into pieces

generous 1½ cups self-rising flour

scant ⅔ cup superfine sugar

4 eggs, beaten

⅔ cup shelled pistachios, chopped

3½ oz/100 g white chocolate, coarsely chopped

confectioners' sugar, for dusting

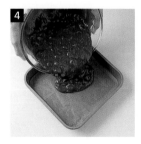

cook's tip

Do not overcook the brownies—they won't be completely firm in the middle when removed from the oven, but will set when they have cooled down.

1 Preheat the oven to 350°/180°C. Grease a 9-inch/23-cm square baking pan and line with parchment paper.

2 Place the chocolate and softened butter in a heatproof bowl set over a pan of simmering water. Stir until melted, then let cool slightly.

3 Sift the flour into a separate bowl and stir in the superfine sugar.

4 Stir the beaten eggs into the chocolate mixture, then pour the mixture into the flour and sugar and beat well. Stir in the pistachios and white chocolate, then pour the mixture into the pan, using a spatula to spread it evenly.

5 Bake in the preheated oven for 30–35 minutes, or until firm to the touch around the edges. Let cool in the pan for 20 minutes. Turn out on to a wire rack. Dust the brownie with confectioners' sugar and let cool completely. Cut into 12 pieces and serve.

rich chocolate loaf

serves 16

prep: 15 mins, (╰
plus 1 hr chilling

cook: 5 mins (╰

*This rich chocolate surprise is incredibly easy to make. Its
presentation as a simple, sliced loaf makes it an ideal idea for
serving to casual guests as a mid-afternoon treat.*

INGREDIENTS

½ cup almonds

5½ oz/150 g semisweet chocolate

6 tbsp unsalted butter

generous ¾ cup sweetened
condensed milk

2 tsp ground cinnamon

2¾ oz/75 g amaretti cookies, broken

1¾ oz/50 g no-soak dried apricots,
coarsely chopped

NUTRITIONAL INFORMATION	
Calories . . . . . . .189 (per slice)	
Protein 3g	
Carbohydrate 18g	
Sugars 18g	
Fat 12g	
Saturates 6g	

variation

Replace the amaretti cookies with
broken graham crackers and the
apricots with the same amount of
raisins, if you like.

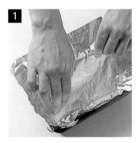

cook's tip

Break the chocolate into
small, manageable pieces
before you heat it in Step 2.
The smaller the pieces, the
quicker it will melt.

1 Line a 1-lb 8-oz/675-g
loaf pan with a sheet
of foil. Coarsely chop the
almonds with a sharp knife
and reserve until required.

2 Place the chocolate,
butter, condensed milk,
and cinnamon in a heavy-

bottomed pan. Place over
low heat, stirring constantly,
for 3–4 minutes, or until the
chocolate has melted.

3 Remove the pan from
the heat and beat the
chocolate mixture well. Stir in
the almonds, cookies, and

apricots with a wooden spoon,
until well mixed.

4 Pour the mixture into
the prepared pan and
chill in the refrigerator for
1 hour, or until set. Cut the
loaf into slices to serve.

zabaglione

serves 6   **prep: 5 mins**   **cook: 10 mins**

This light and frothy, warm dessert which originates from Italy is a welcome treat at the end of a meal. You should serve zabaglione as soon as it is ready, to appreciate its full flavor.

INGREDIENTS

4 egg yolks

⅓ cup superfine sugar

½ cup Marsala wine

amaretti cookies, to serve

NUTRITIONAL INFORMATION	
Calories	110
Protein	2g
Carbohydrate	13g
Sugars	13g
Fat	4g
Saturates	1g

1 Half fill a pan with water and bring to a boil. Reduce the heat so that the water is barely simmering.

2 Beat the egg yolks and sugar with an electric whisk until pale and creamy. Set the bowl over the pan of water. Do not let the bottom touch the surface of the water, or the egg yolks will scramble.

3 Gradually add the Marsala wine, beating constantly with the electric whisk. Continue beating until the mixture is thick and has increased in volume. Pour into heatproof glasses or bowls and serve immediately with amaretti cookies.

cook's tip

Decorate the zabaglione with a slit strawberry, placed on the rim of the glass, or serve with sponge fingers or crisp cookies.

flummery

⏲ cook: 1 hr   ⏱ prep: 10 mins, plus 2–3 hrs cooling/chilling   serves 4

This charming, traditional English desert looks pretty and tastes delicious. It would be a good choice as a cooling dish for a summer dinner party, and should be made well in advance.

NUTRITIONAL INFORMATION	
Calories	544
Protein	6g
Carbohydrate	45g
Sugars	20g
Fat	39g
Saturates	24g

INGREDIENTS

½ cup short-grain rice

1¼ cups milk

1¼ cups heavy cream, plus extra
for decoration

¼ cup superfine sugar

1 tbsp grated lemon rind

1 tsp ground cinnamon, plus
extra for dusting

cook's tip

If you have time, after rinsing the rice, soak it in cold water for 30 minutes, then drain. This helps the grains to absorb the liquid during cooking.

1 Rinse the rice well and place in the top of a double boiler with the milk, cream, sugar, lemon rind, and ground cinnamon. Set over a pan of gently simmering water, cover, and cook, stirring occasionally, for 55 minutes, or until most of the liquid has been absorbed and the rice is tender.

2 Remove the pan from the heat and transfer the rice mixture into individual dishes or cups. Let cool, then cover and chill in the refrigerator for 2–3 hours, or until set.

3 To serve, whip extra heavy cream, decorate each dish with a swirl, and lightly dust with cinnamon.

syllabub

serves 6   **prep: 10 mins,** (L **plus chilling (optional)**   **cook: 0 mins** (L

Wine, brandy, and cream make this old-fashioned dessert wonderfully self-indulgent—and it is guaranteed to make an impression if you serve it at a dinner party.

INGREDIENTS

¾ cup Madeira

2 tbsp brandy

grated rind of 1 lemon

½ cup lemon juice

generous ½ cup superfine sugar

2½ cups heavy cream

10 amaretti cookies or

ratafias, crumbled

ground cinnamon, to dust

lemon slices, to decorate

NUTRITIONAL INFORMATION	
Calories 635	
Protein 3g	
Carbohydrate 31g	
Sugars 31g	
Fat 52g	
Saturates 30g	

1 Whisk the Madeira, brandy, lemon rind, lemon juice, and sugar in a bowl until combined.

2 Add the cream and whisk until the mixture is thick.

3 Divide the cookies between 6 long-stemmed glasses or sundae dishes. Fill each glass or dish with the syllabub mixture and let chill in the refrigerator until ready to serve, if desired. Dust the surface of each dessert with cinnamon and decorate with lemon slices.

cook's tip

Madeira is a fortified wine from the island of the same name. It may be dry, medium, or sweet. Dessert Madeira is best for this recipe—use Bual or Malmsey.

flambéed peaches

⏱ **cook: 5 mins**   ⏱ **prep: 5 mins**   **serves 4**

This dessert is a fabulous end to a dinner party—especially if your guests are watching you cook. It makes a luxurious but, at the same time, refreshing final course.

NUTRITIONAL INFORMATION	
Calories 227	
Protein 3g	
Carbohydrate 26g	
Sugars 26g	
Fat 11g	
Saturates 6g	

INGREDIENTS

3 tbsp unsalted butter

3 tbsp brown sugar

4 tbsp orange juice

4 peaches, peeled, halved, and stoned

2 tbsp amaretto or peach brandy

4 tbsp toasted slivered almonds

cook's tip

Igniting the spirit will burn off the alcohol and mellow the flavor. However, if you are serving this dessert to children, you can omit the amaretto or brandy.

1 Heat the butter, brown sugar, and orange juice in a large, heavy-bottomed skillet over low heat, stirring constantly, until the butter has melted and the sugar has dissolved.

2 Add the peaches and cook for 1–2 minutes on each side, or until golden.

3 Add the amaretto and ignite with a match or taper. When the flames have died down, transfer to serving dishes, sprinkle with toasted slivered almonds, and serve.

sesame bites

serves 4　　　**prep: 15 mins** ⏱　　　**cook: 10–15 mins** ⏱

These delicious, Eastern-style deep-fried treats are crisp and nutty on the outside and melt-in-the-mouth on the inside. Serve them as a special mid-afternoon treat, or as party food.

INGREDIENTS

generous ½ cup sugar

2 tbsp coconut milk

2 eggs, lightly beaten

2 tbsp coconut butter, melted

1¾ cups all-purpose flour

4 tsp shredded unsweetened coconut

¼ tsp baking powder

pinch of salt

4 tbsp sesame seeds

corn oil, for deep-frying

NUTRITIONAL INFORMATION	
Calories	.595
Protein	.11g
Carbohydrate	.80g
Sugars	.32g
Fat	.28g
Saturates	.12g

variation

If you have guests, arrange the bites on a serving plate and dust them with a little confectioners' sugar to serve.

cook's tip

Make sure that you don't add too many of these sesame bites to the hot oil at once, as they will expand a little during cooking.

1 Combine the sugar, coconut milk, eggs, and coconut butter in a bowl. Combine the flour, shredded coconut, baking powder, and salt in a separate bowl, then stir the flour mixture into the egg mixture. Knead lightly until smooth.

2 Form the mixture into small balls with your hands, or with 2 teaspoons. Spread out the sesame seeds on a plate and roll the balls in them to coat.

3 Half-fill a wok or deep, heavy-bottomed skillet with oil and heat to 350–375°F/180–190°C, or until a cube of bread browns in 30 seconds. Add the sesame bites in batches, and deep-fry until golden brown. Remove with a perforated spoon and drain on paper towels. Serve warm.

fried bananas

These wonderfully sticky battered bananas will bring out the child in every member of the family. You could serve them as a special party treat or a late-night snack.

INGREDIENTS

generous ¾ cup all-purpose flour

½ tsp baking soda

pinch of salt

2 tbsp sugar

1 egg

6 tbsp water

1 tbsp sesame seeds

4 bananas

peanut or corn oil, for deep-frying

2 tbsp clear honey, to serve

NUTRITIONAL INFORMATION	
Calories	333
Protein	6g
Carbohydrate	62g
Sugars	38g
Fat	9g
Saturates	1g

variation

You can use the same batter to coat slices of peeled and cored fresh pineapple, and deep-fry them in the same way.

cook's tip

When deep-frying, never leave the skillet unattended and always clean up any spills immediately. Let the fried bananas drain on paper towels to remove any excess oil before serving.

1 Strain the flour into a large bowl with the baking soda and salt. Stir in the sugar, then whisk in the egg and enough of the water to make a smooth, thin batter. Whisk the sesame seeds into the batter.

2 Peel the bananas and halve them lengthwise, then cut each one in half across the center. Heat the oil in a wok or deep, heavy-bottomed skillet to 350–375°F/180–190°C, or until a cube of bread browns in 30 seconds.

3 Dip the banana pieces into the batter to coat, then deep-fry them in batches, until golden brown. Remove the fried bananas with a perforated spoon and drain on paper towels. Transfer to serving plates, drizzle with the honey, and serve.

stuffed nectarines

⏱ **cook: 40–45 mins**   ⏲ **prep: 15 mins**   **serves 6**

NUTRITIONAL INFORMATION	
Calories 260	
Protein 4g	
Carbohydrate 28g	
Sugars 27g	
Fat 10g	
Saturates 4g	

variation

If you prefer, serve with ice cream instead of the whipped cream, and sprinkle the milk chocolate directly over the baked fruit and filling.

This delectable combination of juicy fruit, crunchy amaretti cookies, and bittersweet chocolate is an irresistible summer treat, full of deliciously smooth, complementary flavors.

INGREDIENTS

3 oz/85 g bittersweet chocolate, finely chopped

2 oz/55 g amaretti cookies, crushed into crumbs

1 tsp finely grated lemon rind

white of 1 large egg

6 tbsp amaretto

6 nectarines, halved and pitted

1¼ cups white wine

TO DECORATE

whipped cream

2 oz/55 g milk chocolate, grated

cook's tip

Nectarines are an ideal fruit for stuffing and baking, because they have firm flesh, which holds its shape well during the cooking process.

1 Preheat the oven to 375°F/190°C. Mix the bittersweet chocolate, amaretti cookie crumbs, and lemon rind together in a bowl. Lightly beat the egg white in a clean bowl and add it to the mixture with half the amaretto.

2 Slightly enlarge the nectarine cavities with a small, sharp knife. Add any removed nectarine flesh to the chocolate and crumb mixture and mix well.

3 Arrange the nectarine halves, cut-side up, in an ovenproof dish just large enough to hold them all in a single layer. Divide the chocolate and crumb mixture between them, piling it in the cavities. Mix the wine and remaining amaretto and pour it into the dish around the nectarines.

4 Bake in the preheated oven for 40–45 minutes, or until the nectarines are tender. Transfer 2 nectarine halves to each individual serving plate and spoon over a little of the cooking juices. Serve immediately, decorated with a swirl of whipped cream and a generous sprinkling of grated milk chocolate.

rhubarb & apple crumble

serves 6 **prep: 15 mins** ⏱ **cook: 45 mins** ⏱

In this delicious, warming dessert, a mixture of rhubarb and apples is flavored with orange rind, brown sugar, and cinnamon and covered with a crunchy, hazelnut crumble topping.

INGREDIENTS

1 lb 2 oz/500 g rhubarb

1 lb 2 oz/500 g tart cooking apples

grated rind and juice of 1 orange

½–1 tsp ground cinnamon

scant ½ cup light soft brown sugar

CRUMBLE

generous 1½ cups all-purpose flour

generous ½ cup butter or margarine

scant ⅔ cup light soft brown sugar

⅓ cup toasted chopped hazelnuts

2 tbsp raw brown sugar (optional)

NUTRITIONAL INFORMATION	
Calories 516	
Protein 6g	
Carbohydrate 77g	
Sugars 45g	
Fat 22g	
Saturates 4g	

variation

Any fruits can be topped with crumble. Other flavorings, such as 2 oz/55 g of chopped preserved ginger, can be added to the fruit or crumb mixture.

cook's tip

This crumble can be served cold, if you prefer. Let cool in the dish for 1–2 hours, then serve with a spoonful of whipped cream.

1 Preheat the oven to 400°F/200°C. Cut the rhubarb into 1-inch/2.5-cm lengths and place in a large pan. Peel, core, and slice the apples and add to the rhubarb with the grated orange rind and juice. Bring to a boil, then reduce the heat and simmer for 2–3 minutes, or until the fruit begins to soften.

2 Add the cinnamon and sugar to taste and transfer the mixture to an ovenproof dish. Make sure that the dish is no more than two-thirds full.

3 To make the crumble, sift the flour into a bowl. Add the butter and rub it in until the mixture resembles fine bread crumbs.

Stir in the sugar, then the hazelnuts. Spoon the crumble mixture evenly over the fruit in the dish and smooth the top. Sprinkle with the raw brown sugar, if liked.

4 Cook in the preheated oven for 30–40 minutes, or until the topping is golden brown, then serve.

warm fruit compote

serves 4   **prep: 10 mins** ⟲   **cook: 8–10 mins** ⏱

A bowl of warm summer fruits suffused with exotic spices releases a burst of flavors on to the palate. The velvety syrup is sure to make this fresh, sumptuous dish a firm favorite.

INGREDIENTS

4 plums, halved and stoned

8 oz/225 g raspberries

8 oz/225 g strawberries, hulled and halved

2 tbsp brown sugar

2 tbsp dry white wine

2 star anise

4 cloves

1 cinnamon stick

NUTRITIONAL INFORMATION	
Calories 95	
Protein 2g	
Carbohydrate 21g	
Sugars 21g	
Fat 0g	
Saturates 0g	

1 Place all the ingredients in a large, heavy-bottomed pan. Cook over low heat, stirring occasionally, until the sugar has dissolved.

2 Cover tightly and simmer very gently for 5 minutes, or until the fruit is tender but still retains its shape. Do not let the mixture boil.

3 Remove and discard the star anise, cloves, and cinnamon, and serve the compote warm.

cook's tip

These lightly cooked summer fruits will taste their best if you serve them with a helping of fresh light cream or plain vanilla ice cream.

clafoutis

⏲ **cook: 45 mins**   ⟲ **prep: 15 mins,** **plus 1 hr standing**   **serves 4**

Although the many different recipes for this unusual, batter-based dessert may use a variety of fruits, cherries are the classic filling in Limousin in France, where the dish originated.

NUTRITIONAL INFORMATION	
Calories	297
Protein	7g
Carbohydrate	42g
Sugars	31g
Fat	11g
Saturates	6g

INGREDIENTS

1 lb/450 g sweet black cherries

2 tbsp cherry brandy

1 tbsp confectioners' sugar, plus extra for dusting

butter, for greasing

BATTER

3 tbsp all-purpose flour

3 tbsp sugar

¾ cup light cream

2 eggs, lightly beaten

grated rind of ½ lemon

¼ tsp vanilla extract

cook's tip

Traditionally, in Limousin, the cherries are not pitted before cooking, because the pits are thought to release extra flavor into the dessert.

1 Preheat the oven to 375°F/190°C. Pit the cherries, then place in a bowl with the cherry brandy and confectioners' sugar and mix together. Cover with plastic wrap and let stand for 1 hour.

2 Meanwhile, grease a shallow, ovenproof dish with butter. To make the batter, sift the flour into a bowl and stir in the sugar. Gradually whisk in the light cream, beaten eggs, lemon rind, and vanilla extract. Whisk constantly until the batter is completely smooth.

3 Spoon the cherries into the ovenproof dish and pour the batter over them to cover. Bake in the preheated oven for 45 minutes, or until golden and set. Lightly dust with extra confectioner's sugar and serve warm, or let cool to room temperature before serving.

cinnamon & apricot crêpes

cook: 10 mins   **prep: 15 mins**   **serves 4**

NUTRITIONAL INFORMATION

Calories	.306
Protein	.8g
Carbohydrate	.50g
Sugars	.26g
Fat	.10g
Saturates	.2g

variation

These crêpe pieces are also delicious mixed with 14 oz/400 g of canned morello cherries in syrup, instead of the apricots.

This is a cheap and cheerful, easy-to-make dessert that is perfect for midweek family suppers, and surprisingly filling. Its casual presentation makes it a favorite with children.

INGREDIENTS

2 tbsp superfine sugar

1 tsp ground cinnamon

scant 1 cup all-purpose flour

pinch of salt

2 eggs, lightly beaten

½ cup milk

14 oz/400 g canned apricot halves in syrup

sunflower-seed oil, for brushing

cook's tip

Before you add the batter to the skillet, make sure the oil is very hot. Tilt and roll the skillet as you pour the batter in, to spread it over the bottom in a thin layer.

1 Place the sugar and cinnamon in a bowl, stir to mix, and reserve. Sift the flour and salt into a separate bowl. Whisk the eggs and milk into the flour and continue whisking to make a smooth batter.

2 Drain the apricot halves, reserving the syrup, then whisk the syrup into the batter until combined. Coarsely chop the apricots and reserve.

3 Heat a large crêpe pan or heavy-bottomed skillet and brush with oil. Pour in the batter and cook over medium heat for 4–5 minutes, or until the underside is golden brown. Turn over with a spatula and cook the second side for 4 minutes, or until golden. Tear the crêpe into bite-size pieces with 2 spoons or forks.

4 Add the apricots to the pan and heat through briefly. Divide the crêpe pieces and apricots between individual plates, sprinkle with the sugar and cinnamon mixture, and serve.

spiced syrup sponge

serves 6   **prep: 15 mins**   **cook: 1 hr 30 mins**

Steamed sponges are irresistible on a cold day, but the texture of this dessert is so light it can be served on warm days, too. It makes the ideal finale to a three course meal.

INGREDIENTS

generous ½ cup butter or margarine,
plus extra for greasing

2 tbsp corn syrup, plus extra to serve

scant ⅔ cup superfine sugar

2 eggs

1¼ cups self-rising flour

¾ tsp ground cinnamon

grated rind of 1 orange

1 tbsp orange juice

½ cup golden raisins

1½ oz/40 g preserved ginger,
finely chopped

1 eating apple, peeled, cored, and
coarsely grated

NUTRITIONAL INFORMATION	
Calories	.488
Protein	.5g
Carbohydrate	.78g
Sugars	.56g
Fat	.19g
Saturates	.4g

variation

Substitute light brown sugar for the superfine sugar or allspice for the cinnamon, if you prefer.

cook's tip

You can use an upturned saucer as a trivet when you steam the sponge in Step 5. Keep a pot of boiling water handy for topping up the pan during cooking, otherwise it will boil dry.

1 Thoroughly grease a 3½-cup ovenproof bowl. Pour the corn syrup into the basin.

2 Beat the butter and sugar together until the mixture is light and fluffy and pale in color, then beat in the eggs, one at a time, following each with a spoonful of the flour.

3 Sift in the remaining flour with the cinnamon and fold into the mixture with the orange rind and juice. Fold in the golden raisins, then the ginger and apple.

4 Turn the mixture into the bowl and smooth the top. Cover with a piece of pleated, greased parchment paper, tucking the edges under the rim of the bowl. Cover with a piece of pleated foil. Tie securely in place with string. Tie a piece of string over the top to make a handle.

5 Place the ovenproof bowl on a trivet in a large pan half-filled with boiling water, cover, and steam for 1½ hours, topping up with boiling water as necessary.

6 Remove the bowl from the pan, remove the foil and parchment paper, and turn out on to a warmed serving plate. Serve immediately, in slices, with extra corn syrup.

blueberry compote

serves 6 **prep: 10 mins,** ☾ **plus 2–3 hrs chilling** **cook: 5 mins** ⏲

Serve this easy and attractive dish with whipped cream or ice cream and small, sweet, dessert cookies. It is perfect for entertaining, as it has to be made in advance and chilled.

INGREDIENTS

1 lb 8 oz/675 g blueberries

generous 1⅓ cups superfine sugar

1 tbsp water

2 tbsp gin

dessert cookies, to serve

NUTRITIONAL INFORMATION

Calories 229

Protein 1g

Carbohydrate 57g

Sugars 57g

Fat 0g

Saturates 0g

1 Place the blueberries, superfine sugar, and water in a heavy-bottomed pan over low heat, shaking the pan occasionally, until the sugar has dissolved completely.

2 Remove the pan from the heat and gradually stir in the gin, then let the fruit mixture cool completely.

3 Transfer the compote to dishes, cover, and let chill in the refrigerator for 2–3 hours before serving with dessert cookies.

variation

You can substitute fresh redcurrants for the blueberries and brandy for the gin, if you prefer.

apple fritters

⏲ **cook: 4–6 mins**   ⏱ **prep: 15 mins,**   **serves 4**
plus 30 mins standing

This is a very popular choice for family meals, because children and adults alike love the flavor and crispy texture of the apple rings—and you don't need a spoon or fork to eat them.

NUTRITIONAL INFORMATION	
Calories	.437
Protein	.7g
Carbohydrate	.35g
Sugars	.14g
Fat	.31g
Saturates	.18g

INGREDIENTS

generous ¾ cup all-purpose flour

pinch of salt

2 egg yolks

1 egg white

1 tbsp corn oil

⅔ cup milk

1 lb/450 g cooking apples

juice of 1 lemon

superfine sugar, for sprinkling

½ cup unsalted butter

sour cream, to serve

cook's tip

Choose firm, tart apples for this dish, such as Bramleys or Granny Smith's. Once they are cut, they should be sprinkled with lemon juice immediately and cooked quickly to prevent any discoloration.

1 Sift the flour and salt into a mixing bowl. Make a well in the center and add the egg yolks, egg white, and oil. Gradually incorporate the flour into the liquid with a wooden spoon. Gradually beat in the milk and continue beating to make a smooth batter. Cover with plastic wrap and let stand for 30 minutes.

2 Peel and core the apples, then cut them into rings about ¼-inch/5-mm thick. Spread them out on a plate and sprinkle with the lemon juice and sugar.

3 Melt the butter in a large, heavy-bottomed skillet over medium heat. Dip the apple rings into the batter, one at a time, then drop them into the skillet. Cook for 2–3 minutes on each side, or until golden. Transfer to a serving platter, sprinkle with more sugar and serve with sour cream.

caramelized oranges

serves 6

prep: 25 mins, ⟳
plus 1–2 hrs chilling

cook: 15–20 mins ⟳

These unusual, sugar-coated oranges look almost too pretty to eat—but make sure you do, because they taste wonderfully refreshing, with a real citrus tang.

INGREDIENTS

6 large oranges

5 tbsp water

½ cup superfine sugar

whipped cream, to serve

NUTRITIONAL INFORMATION	
Calories 143	
Protein 2g	
Carbohydrate 35g	
Sugars 35g	
Fat 0g	
Saturates 0g	

cook's tip

For recipes using citrus peel, look for unwaxed specimens—that is, those that have not been treated with diphenyl to preserve their color.

1 Carefully pare wide strips of rind from 2 of the oranges using a swivel-blade vegetable peeler. Cut the strips of rind into thin sticks with a sharp knife and reserve a few for decoration. Peel all the oranges and remove traces of white pith. Cut the fruit horizontally into slices ½-inch/1-cm thick. Place in a serving bowl and tip in any spilt juice.

2 Before making the caramel, half-fill the sink with cold water. Place 3 tablespoons of water and all of the sugar in a heavy-bottomed pan and bring to a boil, stirring constantly, until the sugar has dissolved. Boil, without stirring, until the syrup is a dark caramel color. Remove the pan from the heat and immerse the bottom in the cold water to prevent any additional cooking.

3 Add the remaining 2 tablespoons of water to the pan with the orange rind and simmer over low heat, stirring occasionally, for 8–10 minutes, or until the rind is almost translucent. Pour the mixture over the orange slices, turning them to coat. Cool completely, then chill in the refrigerator for 1–2 hours. Serve with whipped cream, decorated with orange rind.

forest fruits granita

⏲ **cook: 5 mins**   ⏱ **prep: 15 mins, plus 3–4 hrs cooling/freezing**   **serves 4**

This is the perfect dessert for a hot summer's day. It's more cooling and less calorie-packed than ice cream, but is packed with a great combination of fruity flavors.

NUTRITIONAL INFORMATION	
Calories	175
Protein	2g
Carbohydrate	44g
Sugars	44g
Fat	0g
Saturates	0g

INGREDIENTS

8 oz/225 g strawberries, hulled

6 oz/175 g raspberries

6 oz/175 g blackberries, plus extra to decorate

1–2 tbsp lemon juice (optional)

scant ¾ cup superfine sugar

⅔ cup water

TO DECORATE

whipped cream

fresh mint sprigs

variation

For a really lazy granita, replace the fruit paste with 4 cups of fruit juice, such as orange or cranberry juice.

1 Place the strawberries, raspberries, and blackberries in a blender or food processor and process to a paste. Push the paste through a fine-meshed strainer into a freezerproof container to remove the seeds. Add lemon juice to taste.

2 Place the superfine sugar and water in a small pan over low heat and stir until the sugar has dissolved. Pour the syrup over the fruit paste and stir well to combine. Let cool, stirring occasionally, then cover and place in the freezer for 2–3 hours, or until set.

3 Transfer the frozen granita mixture into the refrigerator 30 minutes before serving. Spoon into tall glasses or glass cups and decorate with whipped cream, blackberries, and fresh mint sprigs. Serve.

saucy ice creams

cook: 5–10 mins

prep: 5–10 mins, plus 1 hr cooling/chilling

serves 6

NUTRITIONAL INFORMATION	
Calories . . . . . . .52 / 369 / 103	
Protein . . . . .0 / 2 / 0g	
Carbohydrate . . . .11 / 29 / 10g	
Sugars . . . . .11 / 28 / 7g	
Fat . . . . .0 / 28 / 0g	
Saturates . . . . .0 / 17 / 0g	

variation

You can substitute other fruit, such as pineapple rings or apricots for the apples, if you prefer.

Ice cream is a great freezer standby for dessert, but it can be a little dull and uninspiring. The best way to liven it up is to serve it with a selection of tasty, syrupy sauces.

INGREDIENTS

BERRY SAUCE

8 oz/225 g berries, such as blackberries or raspberries

2 tbsp water

2–3 tbsp superfine sugar

2 tbsp fruit liqueur, such as crème de cassis or crème de framboise

CHOCOLATE SAUCE

⅔ cup heavy cream

¼ cup unsalted butter

¼ cup light brown sugar

6 oz/175 g semisweet chocolate, broken into pieces

2 tbsp rum (optional)

PORT SAUCE

1½ cups ruby port

2 tsp cornstarch

cook's tip

All of the sauces taste spectacular served with plain vanilla ice cream, but ring the changes and try out lots of combinations to find out which sauce you prefer with your favorite flavored ice cream.

1 To make the berry sauce, place all the ingredients in a pan over low heat, stirring occasionally, until the sugar has dissolved and the fruit juices run. Process to a paste with a hand-held blender or in a food processor, then push through a strainer into a bowl to remove the seeds. Add more sugar, if necessary. Serve warm or cold.

2 To make the chocolate sauce, pour the cream into the top of a double boiler and add the butter and sugar. Set over a pan of barely simmering water and stir until smooth. Remove from the heat, let cool slightly, then add the chocolate, stirring until melted. Stir in the rum (if using). Let cool to room temperature before serving.

3 To make the port sauce, place a scant ¼ cup of the port in a bowl with the cornstarch and stir to make a smooth paste. Pour the remainder of the port into a pan and bring to a boil. Stir in the cornstarch paste and cook over high heat, stirring, for 1 minute, or until thickened. Remove the sauce from the heat and let cool. Pour into a bowl, cover, and chill in the refrigerator for 30 minutes before serving.

index

index